NAVIGATING NAFTA

A CONCISE USER'S GUIDE
TO THE NORTH AMERICAN
FREE TRADE AGREEMENT

Barry Appleton, LL.B., LL.M.

Lawyers
Cooperative
Publishing

CARSWELL
Thomson Professional Publishing

The publisher is not engaged in rendering legal, accounting or other professional advice. If legal advice or other expert assistance is required, the services of a competent professional should be sought. The analysis contained herein represents the opinions of the author and should in no way be construed as being official or unofficial policy of any governmental body.

Canadian Cataloguing in Publication Data

Appleton, Barry
    Navigating NAFTA : a concise user's guide to
the North American Free Trade Agreement

Includes index.
ISBN 0-459-55826-9

1. Canada. Treaties, etc. 1922 Oct. 7.
2. Free trade — Canada. 3. Free trade — Mexico.
4. Free trade — United States. 5. Canada —
Commercial treaties. 6. Mexico — Commercial
treaties. 7. United States — Commercial treaties.
I. Title.

HF1766.A77 1994   382'.917   C94-931309-2

The paper used in this publication meets the minimum requirements of the American National Standard for Information Sciences – Permanence of Paper for Printed Library Materials, ANSI X39.48-1984.

 **CARSWELL**
Thomson Professional Publishing

 Lawyers Cooperative Publishing

One Corporate Plaza, 2075 Kennedy Road,	Aqueduct Building
Scarborough, Ontario M1T 3V4	Rochester, New York
Customer Service:	U.S.A. 14694
Toronto: 1-416-609-3800	In the United States, call:
Elsewhere in Canada/U.S. 1-800-387-5164	1-800-527-0430
Fax 1-416-298-5094	

Acknowledgements

First books, like their authors, are beasts which cannot be tamed without the guiding hands of a large number of caring people. This book could never have been produced without the assistance of the following people who generously gave their time and effort. Regine Weston, Ian Peach, Anthony Macri and Joseph Markson all reviewed drafts of this work and endured chronic bouts of author's angst. The Honourable John Roberts also reviewed the text and provided constructive criticism and ongoing encouragement.

A number of individuals provided commentary on various sections of the book. Andreas F. Lowenfeld, the Charles Denison Professor of Law at New York University, kindly provided sage and strategic advice on the dispute settlement chapters and assisted the author in imposing a rigour on sections of this book. Barry Campbell, M.P. took considerable amounts of time from his hectic schedule to review a number of drafts of this book.

Carol Colombo, the Arizona Governor's Special Representative for NAFTA, provided helpful ideas on how this book could better serve the needs of government decision makers. Professor Ellie Perkins of York University and Jim Grieshaber-Otto from the government of British Columbia both provided important ideas regarding the impact of the NAFTA on governmental policy capacity. Toronto environmental lawyer, Charles Birchall, also provided thoughtful input throughout the writing of the book, as did author Hargurchet Bhabra.

Nancy Marto made heroic efforts in editing this text and in reviewing its galleys. As well, Paul Elliot assisted in the creation of the title of this book. Two members of the Canadian and American bars made important contributions to this work. The author considers himself fortunate to have been able to call upon the expertise of financial services lawyer Jeffrey Graham. David Kerzner, B.A., LL.B, LL.M., also provided counsel and criticism at key moments during the writing of the book.

To my colleagues at the Ontario Ministry of Intergovernmental Affairs, I owe special thanks. They provided ongoing opportunities to assess the deeper meaning of the NAFTA in the context of public policy making. I would like especially to acknowledge those people with whom I had the pleasure to work in this area over the past few years: Claude Galipeau, Frank Longo, Michal Ben-Gera, Paul Barber, Bill Forward, Alvaro del Castillo, Larry Kent and Despy Whyte-Simms. I hasten to add that this book reflects the author's own views. It should not be construed as constituting legal advice and does not necessarily constitute or reflect the views of the Ministry of Intergovernmental Affairs or the government of Ontario.

Professor K. Venkata Raman of the Faculty of Law at Queen's University first provided this author with a forum to discuss the meanings of free trade agreements. His support and influence have made the discussions within this book possible. Professor John D. Whyte also played a formative role in the discussions leading to the constitutional sections of this book. In addition, the ongoing support of Senator D. Keith Davey has also been reassuring and of strategic benefit.

Thanks are owed to the fine team of Thompson Professional Publishing. In Canada, special thanks must go to John Edmiston, who was able to get this project moving and Dianne Overholt, who worked tirelessly on the marketing of this project. Reina Zatylny edited this book masterfully, ably bringing this project together quickly, effectively and professionally.

Special thanks is due for the efforts of Julie Chan, who provided encouragement and direction throughout this project. I also would like to acknowledge the ongoing support of my family, in particular, the encouragement that I received from Percy Lederman, Dr. Nancy Wiederhorn and my father, Dr. Sherwood Appleton.

This book is dedicated to the memory of the late Harold Siegal, a fine civil litigator and early mentor, whose presence touched many and whose loss touched us all. This book would never have come about without his early encouragement. *Vixere fortes ante Agamemnona.*

Table of Contents

Table of Cases

References are to page numbers

1
Overview

There is a tide in the affairs of men,
Which, taken at the flood, leads on to fortune;
Omitted, all the voyage of their life
Is bound in shallows and in miseries.
On such a full sea are we now afloat;
And we must take the current when it serves,
Or lose our ventures.

Shakespeare, *Julius Caesar,*
V:iii

On January 1, 1994, a tide of economic change swept North America and with its flood reshaped the economic map of the continent. The North American Free Trade Agreement (NAFTA) establishes a single trade zone comprising nearly 360 million people. While not creating a full-fledged "Common Market"[1], the NAFTA creates a free trade zone in goods and will significantly liberalize the treatment of investment, intellectual property and services across the continent.

While the debate raged in national capitals regarding the economic, social, cultural and philosophical impact of the Agreement, negotiators for each country carefully attempted to reach consensus over those complex clauses which now govern aspects of trade on the continent. As in many other areas, trade law and policy has developed its own specialized language which serves to distance non-specialists from the meaning locked away within these agreements. Thus, the goal of this book is to unlock the meaning of the NAFTA and, where possible, make it understandable. This book seeks to provide a concise, unbiased and accurate account of what is contained in the NAFTA. It describes and explains the elements of this new kind of Agreement which governs nearly all aspects of trade in goods and services on the continent. Wherever possible, the NAFTA will be examined

---

1 All common markets display four fundamental freedoms: freedom of goods, services, capital and labour. The NAFTA will lead to a free market in goods, and liberalizes the markets for services and capital. It does not create a free market for services, capital or labour.

in the light of other international agreements to see if they can provide some insight into its terms. In addition, where it appears clear that a provision is capable of multiple meanings, the wording will be identified, and the provision will be clearly marked to indicate those areas where future disagreements are likely.

While stating what this book does, it is also important to clearly set out what this book does not do. This book does not focus deeply on the political, philosophical, economic or social impact of the Agreement. That is left to the capable hands of historians, political scientists and economists. What this book attempts to do is make the NAFTA more accessible. Judgments on the ultimate meaning of the Agreement can then be left entirely to the reader.

This book provides a chapter-by-chapter guide to the NAFTA's 22 chapters and its Supplemental Agreements. It also examines a series of commonly raised questions regarding the NAFTA. This book attempts to distil and explain the underlying themes which permeate the Agreement and which will become important in the new North American economy. In conclusion, it is only with foresight and knowledge that the citizens of NAFTA countries will be able to "take the current when it serves" so as not to lose their way as they navigate the NAFTA.

1. WHAT IS THE NAFTA?

The North American Free Trade Agreement is an international treaty negotiated between the governments of Mexico, the United States and Canada. The Agreement itself comprises a text of more than 1,000 pages. In addition, the NAFTA is supported by the following material:

- domestic legislation which was used to implement the NAFTA obligations into domestic law in Canada and the United States[2];

- Supplemental Agreements to the NAFTA on the environment and labour and the trilateral understanding on emergency actions, signed on September 14, 1993;

- letters by NAFTA Parties which clarify or modify provisions in the Agreement;

- the *Statement of Administrative Action* produced by the American Administration which sets out its position regarding the implementation of the NAFTA[3];

---

2 International treaties are the supreme law of Mexico and as such, implementing legislation is not required *per se*.
3 H.R. Doc No. 159, 103d. Cong. 1st Sess. v.1 (1993).

- *Statement of Government Action* issued by the Canadian government which sets out its position on key NAFTA implementation and interpretive questions[4];

- regulations of NAFTA Parties dealing with the Agreement; and

- the rulings of panels on the provisions of the General Agreement on Tariffs and Trade[5] (GATT) and the Canada-U.S. Free Trade Agreement[6] which have been incorporated into the NAFTA.

2. BACKGROUND TO THE NAFTA

What would this island be without foreign trade, but a
place of confinement to the inhabitants, who (without it)
could be but a kind of Hermites, as being separated
from the rest of the world; it is foreign trade that
renders us rich, honourable and great, that gives us a
name and esteem in the world.

Charles Molloy,
De Jure Maritimo et Navale, 1676[7].

Even before these words were written in the 17th century, countries had seen the benefits in international trade. However, the politics of trade have changed fundamentally from the 17th century, as they have from the first days of the General Agreement on Tariffs and Trade in 1948. Trade had been the domain of diplomats who focussed on questions regarding tariffs. This preoccupation with tariff reduction could not extend to liberalizing access on other issues such as trade in services, the reduction of non-tariff barriers, subsidies and dumping of goods or intellectual property. During the half century which has nearly passed since the creation of the GATT, significant changes have occurred in global markets. Increasingly, local matters have become connected with global trade decisions to the point where issues regarding local health standards or environmentally friendly fishing practices can become international issues.

Besides having its roots in the GATT, the NAFTA was greatly influenced by the United States' first bilateral trade and services agreement, the United States-Israel Free Trade Agreement[8] and its second, the Canada-

---

4   *Canada Gazette*, Part II, Jan. 1, 1994.

5   55 U.N.T.S. 194, GATT, BISD, 1st Supp. 6 (1953).

6   1989 C.T.S. 3, H.R. Doc. No. 216, 100th Cong., 2d Sess. 297 (1988).

7   Cited by Clive Schmitthoff in *Schmitthoff's Export Trade*, 7th ed. (London: Stevens & Sons, 1980), title page.

8   U.S.-Israel Free Trade Agreement, Jan. 1, 1985, 24 I.L.M. 301.

U.S. Free Trade Agreement. In particular, the Canada-U.S. Free Trade Agreement provided the basis for many of the NAFTA's 22 chapters. This similarity can be confusing. Indeed, during the legislative hearings on the NAFTA in Canada, a senior Canadian official compared the earlier agreement to the NAFTA by saying[9]:

> To a large extent, the bill duplicates what the FTA enacted; it just uses different terminology — it talks about NAFTA as an FTA. . . . Substantively, the only area that is really new involves the intellectual property provisions.

However, while the NAFTA built upon the framework set up by the Canada-U.S. Free Trade Agreement, this book will show that the NAFTA is a fundamentally different document. Thus, in order to understand what the NAFTA means, it is not enough to merely rely upon that earlier bilateral treaty. One must look at the NAFTA itself.

3. WHY IS THE NAFTA IMPORTANT?

The NAFTA is a milestone development in the negotiation of international trade agreements. These developments occur in a number of areas:

- The NAFTA is the first trade agreement of its kind which integrates the economies of developed and developing countries. Other agreements have not been able to come to terms with the same level of obligation on issues such as standard setting, investment and services. This has required the NAFTA negotiators to grapple with issues which had not been canvassed by earlier trade treaties such as the GATT or the Canada-U.S. Free Trade Agreement.

- The NAFTA creates a significant enhancement in the scope and application of comprehensive trade agreements dealing with goods, services and investment. The NAFTA moved away from an approach based on individual listings of each covered area, to a sectoral approach that only lists areas which are not covered. As a result, not only is the NAFTA an agreement of wide sweep but it is one of great policy depth.

- The NAFTA breaks new ground for international agreements by creating an ability for individual investors to challenge governments before international arbitral tribunals if a NAFTA investment obligation has been impaired. The increase in number of potential

---

9 *Hansard*, Minutes of the Proceedings and Evidence of the House of Commons Legislative Committee on Bill C-115, April 27, 1993, vol. 2, at 12. Testimony of Konrad von Finckenstein, Assistant Deputy Attorney General of Canada, Tax Law Branch, Department of Justice.

litigants from three countries imparts a unique character to this Agreement.

• The NAFTA openly acknowledges the link between trade and the environment. This direct linkage, while not sufficient for many, will likely become the new minimum standard of treatment for future international trade agreements. However, while this link was made, other links between trade and policy areas such as human rights or social policy have not been made clear.

These trends have not gone unnoticed and they have been both lauded and denounced in each of the NAFTA countries. Without doubt, the NAFTA has become an important economic charter which will have an ongoing impact upon the economic, legislative, social and legal development of its Parties for a considerable time to come.

2

Implementing the NAFTA

1. BRINGING INTERNATIONAL AGREEMENTS INTO FORCE

In order for treaties to become binding, they must be brought into force. Bringing a treaty into force usually occurs in three stages: signature, domestic implementation and the deposit of the instrument of ratification. Countries initially indicate their assent to an agreement by signing it. This does not make the agreement binding on that country, it merely indicates that the country agrees with the principles in that treaty.

Signatories are then presented with the need to give the agreement the force of law within their state. There are three approaches to the domestic implementation of treaties:

(1) incorporating international agreements into domestic law and giving precedence to international treaties over domestic law[1];

(2) requiring that treaties be considered by a legislative body and that once that body has approved the agreement, it will become binding[2]; and

(3) requiring that domestic laws be modified to the extent to which they conflict with treaty obligations[3].

Once domestic implementation is complete, a country will take the final step of communicating its readiness by "depositing" an "instrument of ratification". This indicates that the country is ready to undertake the obligations of the treaty[4]. This requirement is usually set out in the treaty itself. For example, the NAFTA provides that it came into "force on January

---

1 These are known as monist states. International law immediately becomes the supreme law and all domestic laws must immediately conform.

2 For example, once the Mexican Senate has ratified a treaty, it becomes the supreme law of Mexico and no domestic implementation is required.

3 Both Canada and the United States require the implementation of international treaties in domestic law.

4 In some multilateral treaties, there is a final step of waiting for a minimum number of ratifications before the treaty becomes valid.

1, 1994 on an exchange of written notifications certifying the completion of necessary legal procedures"[5].

The NAFTA is an agreement between three federal states: Canada, the United States and Mexico. Because of differences in the internal distribution of constitutional authority between the NAFTA Parties, each Party has a different procedure for the implementation of treaties.

(a) CANADA

In Canada, the federal government has jurisdiction over the negotiation of international treaties. Authority over the implementation of treaties in Canada is not as straightforward. When Canada received its independence from Great Britain in 1867, the new government did not receive the power over international affairs. While the *Constitution Act, 1867* spoke of a federal power to implement Imperial Treaties[6], it did not consider the eventuality that one day Canada could negotiate its own treaties. Thus in 1931, when the government of Canada received the authority to have its own foreign policy[7], the issue of whether it could implement its new treaties was left open.

Once the federal government has entered into an international agreement, it need not obtain Parliamentary approval for it[8]. Further, if the agreement only deals with matters within the authority of the executive branch of government, no further implementation need be taken. If the agreement requires legislative changes, only then will implementing legislation be placed before Parliament. However, should the subject matter of the agreement be beyond the legislative jurisdiction of the federal government, then Parliament alone will be incapable of fully implementing the agreement. In this situation, enabling legislation must be passed in each province to complete the agreement's implementation. This split in authority to implement international agreements is an integral part of Canadian federalism.

---

5   NAFTA article 2203.
6   Section 132 of the *Constitution Act, 1867* reads:
    The Parliament and Government of Canada shall have all Powers necessary or proper for performing the Obligations of Canada or any Province thereof, as Part of the British Empire, towards Foreign Countries, arising under Treaties between the Empire and such Foreign Countries.
7   *Statute of Westminster, 1931*, (U.K.) 22 Geo. V, c. 4.
8   This is a key difference between the Canadian and the American systems.

(i) The Division of Powers

In the *Labour Conventions* case[9], the Privy Council was asked to rule on whether the Canadian federal government could pass domestic legislation to implement a treaty in an area of provincial jurisdiction. The court ruled that the federal government did not have the jurisdiction to implement a treaty in that area. The decision of the Privy Council established that, in the absence of a treaty power, the authority to implement treaties falls to that government which has the appropriate jurisdiction for the subject-matter covered in that agreement. This requires that a determination be made whether an international agreement is a matter which is, in pith and substance, within the jurisdiction of the federal or provincial government. If it is entirely within the federal government's jurisdiction, then no provincial implementation legislation is required. If the agreement is in an area of provincial jurisdiction, then there will be portions of the agreement which remain unimplemented in Canada until the provinces pass appropriate implementing legislation.

In order to ascertain whether the NAFTA is within the jurisdiction of the government of Canada, it is necessary to look at the distribution of powers in the Canadian system. Authority is split between the federal and provincial government on the basis of ss. 91 to 95 of the *Constitution Act, 1867*, with each level of government having the exclusive power to legislate within its subject areas.

(A) *Federal Powers*

The Constitution grants specific powers to the government of Canada, including such areas as: tariffs[10], national marketing standards[11], intellectual property[12] and banking.[13] It also provides general powers for peace, order and good government[14] and trade and commerce[15].

Section 91 of the *Constitution Act, 1867* contains a general power for the federal government to maintain the peace, order and good government of the state[16]. This power has been used by the federal government to regulate areas of the economy and the general welfare of the state. The POGG power has been reviewed by the courts in a number of cases. These courts have identified three areas where the POGG power can be used: for

---

9 *Canada (A.G.) v. Ontario (A.G.)* (*Labour Conventions* case), [1937] A.C. 326 (P.C.).
10 *Constitution Act, 1867*, s. 91(3).
11 *Constitution Act, 1867*, s. 91(17).
12 *Constitution Act, 1867*, ss. 91(22) and 91(23).
13 *Constitution Act, 1867*, ss. 91(15) and 91(16).
14 *Constitution Act, 1867*, s. 91.
15 *Constitution Act, 1867*, s. 91(2).
16 This power is often referred to by its initials as the POGG power.

new areas where there is no constitutional jurisdiction[17], for emergency situations and for national concerns. It is to this last area that an agreement such as the NAFTA would be most closely associated.

In an early case, the *Local Prohibitions case*[18], the Privy Council found that there was an ability for the federal government to legislate in areas of national importance only where it could be clearly established that the dimensions of the activity being legislated were not of a local and private nature, but were truly of "national dimensions". The national dimensions test was somewhat modified by the Supreme Court of Canada in *Reference Re Natural Products Marketing Act*[19]. It augmented the test by allowing only those subjects which are within the jurisdiction of the Parliament of Canada to be matters of national concern. In its recent decision in *R. v. Crown Zellerbach Can. Ltd.*[20], the Supreme Court of Canada established that the national concern branch of POGG could apply to "matters which although originally matters of a local or private nature in a province, have since . . . become matters of national concern"[21]. Justice Le Dain, speaking for the majority, established two guidelines for national concerns under POGG. He stated[22]:

> For a matter to qualify as a matter of national concern . . . it must have a singleness, distinctiveness and indivisibility that clearly distinguishes it from matters of provincial concern and a scale of impact on provincial jurisdiction that is reconcilable with the fundamental distribution of legislative power under the Constitution.

> In determining whether a matter has attained the required degree of singleness, distinctiveness and indivisibility that clearly distinguishes it from matters of provincial concern, it is relevant to consider what would be the effect on extra-provincial interests of a provincial failure to deal effectively with the control or regulation of the intra-provincial aspects of the matter.

It is uncertain whether this national concern test would justify federal authority over the unilateral implementation of the NAFTA. There are a number of criteria that the NAFTA may not comply with. For example, it is possible that the NAFTA would not comply with the indivisibility aspect of the *Zellerbach* test as its provisions could be severable. As well, it would be up to a future court to assess how one could reconcile the reduction of provincial authority caused by the NAFTA with the division of powers.

---

17 While this area has been identified, it is not entirely certain that "newness" constitutes an area unto itself under the POGG power.

18 *Ontario (A.G.) v. Canada (A.G.)* (*Local Prohibition* case), [1896] A.C. 348 at 361.

19 [1936] S.C.R. 398.

20 [1988] 1 S.C.R. 401.

21 Per Le Dain, J. at 432.

22 At 432.

The federal government could try to base its implementation of the NAFTA on its trade and commerce power. The *Constitution Act, 1867* grants a broad power to the federal government under s. 91(2). This wide power was quickly constrained by the Privy Council in *Citizens' Insurance Co. v. Parsons*[23]. Sir Montague Smith, speaking for their Lordships, stated[24]:

> Construing therefore the words "regulation of trade and commerce" by the various aids to their interpretation above suggested, they would include political arrangements in regard to trade requiring the sanction of Parliament, regulation of trade in matters of inter-provincial concern, and it may be that they would include general regulation of trade affecting the whole dominion.

The second branch of the *Parsons* test, dealing with national dimensions, has been maintained in a number of subsequent cases[25]. This test has been clarified by the Supreme Court of Canada in *City National Leasing Ltd. v. General Motors of Can. Ltd.*[26]. In his majority decision, Chief Justice Dickson established five elements as the basis of the valid federal exercise of the national dimensions branch of the trade and commerce power:[27]

(1) the presence of a national regulatory scheme;

(2) the oversight of a regulatory agency;

(3) a concern with trade in general rather than with an aspect of a particular business;

(4) whether the provinces jointly and severally would be constitutionally incapable of passing such an enactment; and

(5) the failure to include one or more provinces or localities would jeopardize the successful operation in other parts of the country.

The Chief Justice pointed out a critical issue in this case. He stated that courts must reconcile the federal trade and commerce power against the provincial power over property and civil rights. This is a task which Chief Justice Dickson conceded will not be easy to balance[28].

Thus the federal government has broad general powers, in addition to its specific constitutional grants of authority, under which it could attempt to justify the implementation of a trade agreement like the NAFTA. However, none of the recent cases of the Supreme Court which have expanded

---

23 (1881), 7 App. Cas. 96.

24 At 109.

25 *Toronto Electric Commissioners v. Snider*, [1925] A.C. 396; *John Deere Plow Co. v. Wharton*, [1915] A.C. 330; *Re Board of Commerce Act, 1919 (Canada)* (1920), 60 S.C.R. 456; *MacDonald v. Vapour Canada Ltd.*, [1977] 2 S.C.R 134 and *A.G. (Can.) v. C.N. Tpt. Co.*, [1983] 2 S.C.R. 206.

26 [1989] 1 S.C.R. 641 at 662.

27 *General Motors v. City National Leasing*, at 662.

28 Per Dickson C.J.C. at 659.

these general powers, has overturned the *Labour Conventions* case. Without overturning this seminal decision, the federal government will need to demonstrate that the NAFTA is a matter within its jurisdiction before its unilateral implementation will be constitutionally valid.

(B) *Provincial Powers*

The *Constitution Act, 1867* grants extensive powers to the Canadian provinces for matters such as property and civil rights within the province[29], matters of a local or private nature[30], most areas of labour[31], education[32], and health care[33], consumer protection[34], insurance[35], trusts, securities, licensing and investment[36]. Because of the scope and depth of the NAFTA, all of these areas of provincial jurisdiction will be affected by the obligations contained within the Agreement.

(ii) Parliamentary Implementation

The Parliament of Canada introduced implementing legislation for the NAFTA on February 25, 1993. This bill was passed by the House of Commons and Senate and was given Royal Assent on June 23, 1993[37]. The *North American Free Trade Agreement Implementation Act* was proclaimed into force on January 1, 1994[38].

No province has passed legislation to implement the Agreement. Because of the nature of the Canadian federation, some provinces disagreed with the federal implementation. At the time of writing, Canada's most industrialized province, Ontario, has announced that it will challenge the constitutionality of the Canadian federal government's implementation of the NAFTA[39].

---

29 *Constitution Act, 1867*, s. 92(13).
30 *Constitution Act, 1867*, s. 92(16).
31 The *Snider* case established general provincial authority. In *Re Industrial Relations and Disputes Investigation Act*, [1955] S.C.R. 529, the Supreme Court upheld the federal government authority to regulate labour in areas under its exclusive jurisdiction such as navigation and shipping.
32 *Constitution Act, 1867*, s. 93.
33 *Constitution Act, 1867*, s. 92(7).
34 *Shannon v. British Columbia (Lower Mainland Dairy Product Board)*, [1938] A.C. 708.
35 This was decided by the *Parsons* case.
36 *Constitution Act, 1867*, s. 92(13).
37 *North American Free Trade Agreement Implementation Act*, S.C. 1993, c. 44.
38 *Canada Gazette*, Part II, Jan. 12, 1994, SI/94-1.
39 Statement of Premier Bob Rae to the Ontario Legislature, *Hansard*, Oct. 13, 1993 at 3419.

(b) UNITED STATES

Under the United States Constitution, the federal government has plenary authority over the conduct of foreign affairs[40]. While an agreement like the NAFTA is certainly a matter of federal jurisdiction, the extent to which it is within the authority of the executive or legislative branch of government can be the subject of some debate. Congress has the general authority to make laws[41] and the specific authority to regulate trade with foreign nations[42]. At the same time, the President has wide powers over foreign policy. Professor John Jackson has written that[43]:

> The *United States* v. *Curtis Wright Export Co.*, even propounded the theory that the United States President has certain inherent powers over foreign affairs that do not depend on the Constitution! Although many scholars reject this theory, for practical reasons the presidency has developed a preeminent role in the conduct of U.S. foreign affairs.

While it is difficult to draw the line between the exclusive zones of authority between branches of government, it is clear that for an agreement like the NAFTA the consent of both the executive and legislative branches of government is required.

The NAFTA was implemented through a special congressional process known as Fast Track[44]. Through this process, Congress agrees to limit its power to amend international trade agreements and to vote on such legislation on a very short schedule. Timing is essential under Fast Track and is determined around three milestone events:

(1) notification by the President that trade negotiations will begin;
(2) signing of a trade agreement by the President; and
(3) transmittal of the agreement with implementing legislation to Congress.

The first of these milestones was achieved by President George Bush. The President notified Congress on September 25, 1990 of his intention to negotiate a trade agreement with Mexico. Later, on February 5, 1991, he further notified Congress that Canada would join these negotiations.

The second milestone was passed on December 17, 1992, when President Bush, Mexican President Carlos Salinas and Canadian Prime Minister Brian Mulroney signed the final text of the NAFTA. This fulfilled the

---

40 *United States* v. *Curtis-Wright Export Corp.*, 299 U.S. 304 (1936).
41 U.S. Const. art. I, §8, cl. 18.
42 US Const. art. I, §8, cl. 3.
43 John Jackson, *The World Trading System: Law and Policy of International Economic Relations* (Cambridge, Mass.: MIT Press, 1991) at 61.
44 Fast Track was first provided by §§101-102 of the *Trade Act of 1974*, 19 U.S.C. §§2101, 2111-2112, 2191 (1988).

second requirement of Fast Track. Upon initialling, Congress was given 90 calender days to consider and review the text with the American Administration. Only after this period of time elapsed could the President formally sign the Agreement.

After the signing of the Agreement, the President was obliged to send to Congress a copy of the Agreement, an implementing bill and a *Statement of Administrative Action*. Under Fast Track, Congress was required to hold a yes or no vote on the legislation as submitted. This vote had to occur within 60 Congressional sitting days of the Agreement's introduction.

In order to enhance the possibility of Congressional ratification of the trade agreement, the adminstration actively consulted with members of Congress through "mock mark-ups" of the NAFTA implementing legislation. These unofficial drafts of the Agreement's implementing legislation were shared by the Administration with the legislative branch of government. It was through these unofficial documents that the Adminstration could gauge its support for the Agreement. It is also at this time that potential legislative amendments are considered, for once the "mock mark-ups" are submitted as implementing legislation no changes may occur.

The Clinton Administration transmitted the NAFTA formally to the House of Representatives as House Resolution 3250 on October 4, 1993. The implementation of the NAFTA resulted in a colourful show of congressional antics and executive largesse. Night after night, American news commentators speculated on the President's ability to push the Agreement through Congress over the opposition of a considerable number of members of Congress. On November 17, 1993, the House of Representatives passed the NAFTA bill by a vote of 234 to 200. On November 19, the Senate passed the same legislation[45]. The NAFTA was proclaimed into law in the United States on January 1, 1994 by President Bill Clinton[46].

(c) MEXICO

Of all the NAFTA Parties, Mexico was under the greatest pressure to amend its laws to make them consistent with the NAFTA. Large sections of the NAFTA were negotiated on account of the absence of certain laws in Mexico relating to issues like intellectual property, GATT government procurement obligations, transparency procedures and civil remedies like injunctions.

Under Mexican law, the President has the power to negotiate treaties, but before they come into force, all treaties must be ratified by a two-thirds

---

45 This bill became the *North American Free Trade Agreement Implementation Act* (Public Law 103-182, 107 Stat. 2057).

46 58 FR 69681, Executive Order 12889 of Dec. 27, 1993.

vote of the Senate and by a majority in the Chamber of Deputies[47]. Both the Chamber and the Senate passed the NAFTA by an overwhelming majority in November, 1993. Once ratified, and published in the Diario Oficial, the NAFTA became the supreme law of the land[48]. Since the fall of 1993, Mexico has amended a number of its domestic laws to implement its NAFTA commitments, especially those relating to investment and intellectual property.

2. EXTENT OF OBLIGATION

One of the most basic rules of international law is that nations must uphold their international agreements[49]. The international commitments entered into by national governments are binding upon them under international law and custom. The NAFTA is an agreement that places significant obligations on its "Parties". The Parties to the NAFTA are the federal governments of the United States, Canada and Mexico. While the distribution of constitutional authority in each of the NAFTA Parties is different, each Party has undertaken obligations in areas that are regulated by subnational governments, that is, state, provincial and local governments. In order to ensure that the obligations of the NAFTA were not evaded by subnational measures, the Agreement contains provisions setting out the extent of obligations of Parties to compel adherence by subnational governments.

(a) NAFTA PROVISIONS ON EXTENT OF OBLIGATION

Extent of obligation clauses are contained in the GATT, the Canada-U.S. Free Trade Agreement and the NAFTA. It is important to view the NAFTA provision in the context of similar provisions in these other agreements. GATT Article XXIV:12 sets out its extent of obligation language. It states:

> Each contracting party shall take such reasonable measures as may be available to it to ensure observance of the provisions of this Agreement by the regional and local governments and authorities within its territory.

The NAFTA takes a slightly different approach. NAFTA article 105 mirrors article 103 of the Canada-U.S. Free Trade Agreement by stating:

---

47 Ley sobre la Celebración de Tratados [Law of Treaties]. Diario Oficial de la Federación, (Jan. 1, 1992), article 4.
48 Mexican Constitution, article 133.
49 This is known as the rule of *pacta sunt servanda* and is reflected in article 26 of the *Vienna Convention on the Law of Treaties*, 1969.

The Parties shall ensure that all necessary measures are taken in order to give effect to the provisions of this Agreement including their observance, except as otherwise provided in this Agreement, by state, provincial and local governments.

While the wording of the NAFTA and Canada-U.S. Free Trade Agreement clauses is identical, there will likely be a difference in the meaning of the sections. This is due to the difference in coverage caused by negative and positive listing. The Canada-U.S. Free Trade Agreement followed a "positive listing process". That is, for the agreement to impose an obligation on a Party, a specific subject was required to be listed within the Agreement[50]. The NAFTA took a different route by using a "negative listing process". When a subject was listed in the NAFTA, all matters were covered unless they were specifically exempted. Negative listing creates substantially greater obligations under the NAFTA than under the Canada-U.S. Free Trade Agreement.

There is only one exception to this general provincial obligation clause: the Technical Standards chapter. Article 902 of that chapter states that the general extent of obligation clause does not apply to Articles 904 through 908. Instead, this section reads:

Each Party shall seek, through appropriate measures, to ensure observance of Articles 904 through 908 by provincial or state governments and by non-governmental standardizing bodies in its territory.

The NAFTA drafters chose wording which differed from the Canada-U.S. Free Trade Agreement and the GATT extent of obligation language. As the term "appropriate measures" has never been interpreted in the international trade context, its full legal meaning remains somewhat unclear in the absence of arbitral rulings. One could surmise that the obligation here is weaker than that in the rest of the NAFTA and that this wording resembles the "reasonable measures" obligation which is the basis of the extent of obligation language in the GATT[51]. Presumably state, provincial and local governments will have greater discretionary ambit in dealing with standards issues than they would otherwise have under the NAFTA.

(b) CANADA

The NAFTA established international obligations upon the government of Canada. Since the provinces are not Parties to the Agreement, they have no direct obligation to follow the policies contained within it. This leaves

---

50 For example, the financial service obligations under the Canada-U.S. Free Trade Agreement were highly restricted to specified areas.

51 GATT Article XXIV:12.

open to question the extent to which the NAFTA obligations will be enforceable on the Canadian provinces. Federal responsibility for the maintenance of treaty obligations was established by the Supreme Court of Canada in the 1967 *Offshore Minerals Reference*[52]. The court held that the federal government owned the offshore mineral rights off the British Columbia coast. The court stated[53]:

> It is Canada, not the province of British Columbia, that will have to answer the claims of other members of the international community for breach of the obligations and responsibilities imposed by the Convention.

From this case, it is clear that under the NAFTA, the Canadian federal government will be responsible for any NAFTA-inconsistent actions which take place in Canada. What is not clear, is whether the Canadian federal government has the constitutional authority to remedy such a situation.

Historically, a co-operative process has occurred in Canada where the federal government has been able to obtain the consent of provinces to international agreements where such consent was required. However, situations have occurred where provinces have opposed the ability of the federal government to implement treaties on the basis that this would allow the federal government to usurp their jurisdiction by way of an international treaty in a way not allowed under the constitution[54]. In its *Statement of Government Action*, the Canadian federal government has alluded to its desire to have cooperative implementation of the NAFTA. It stated[55]:

> The federal government anticipates that in the interests of the Canadian economy, provincial governments will themselves ensure that their legislation and regulations are consistent with the Agreement.

Notwithstanding any jurisdictional uncertainty which is presented by the NAFTA, the Parliament of Canada has implemented the Agreement. To deal with the extent of obligation issue, s. 9 of the legislation contains the following section[56]:

> For greater certainty, nothing in the Act, by specific mention or ommission, limits in any manner the right of Parliament to enact legislation to implement any provision of the Agreement or fulfil any obligation of the Government of Canada under the Agreement.

---

52 *Re Offshore Mineral Rights of British Columbia*, [1967] S.C.R. 792.
53 At 821.
54 This was the issue raised in the *Labour Conventions* case, [1937] A.C. 326 (P.C.).
55 *Statement of Government Action* at 79.
56 *North American Free Trade Agreement Implementation Act*, S.C. 1993, s. 9.

The *Statement of Government Action* expands upon the meaning of this section. It states[57]:

> Section 9 states that Parliament considers that it has the legislative authority to implement the entire Agreement. It reserves to Parliament the right to make full use of such authority, when necessary, to ensure that Canadian obligations arising from the Agreement are respected.

While this provision purports to give the government of Canada the ability to fulfil its obligations under the NAFTA, its constitutionality remains uncertain at this time.

(c) UNITED STATES

Federal law, which includes federal treaties and congressional statutes, are the supreme law of the United States[58]. In the case of inconsistency, federal law will preempt state law[59]. The Constitution does not establish any paramountcy rules between federal treaty law and federal statutes. On this question, the Supreme Court has ruled that the most recent provision will be paramount[60].

While the North American Free Trade Agreement is an international agreement, it is not a treaty, but an executive agreement. Court decisions have determined that for the purposes of the Supremacy Clause, executive agreements are treated like other federal laws in that they can preclude inconsistent state law[61].

The GATT is an example of an executive agreement dealing with international trade. A recent GATT panel decision has looked at the relationship of state laws to federal executive agreements[62]. In this case regarding American wine and beer practices, Canada argued that state tax and distribution laws unfairly discriminated against competition from Canadian brewers. The GATT panel report found for Canada and stated that "GATT law is part of federal law in the United States and as such is superior to GATT-inconsistent state law"[63]. This issue was also raised in a recent

---

57 *Statement of Government Action* at 79.

58 U.S. Const. art. VI, §2. Treaties made under the authority of the United States are the supreme law of the land. This was also made clear by the Supreme Court in *Missouri* v. *Holland*, 252 U.S. 416 (1920) at 432-433.

59 There is a good discussion of this area of law in chapter 9 of Louis Henkin, *Foreign Affairs and the Constitution* (Mineola, New York: Foundation Press, 1972).

60 *Chae Chan Ping* v. *United States (Chinese Exclusion case)*, 130 U.S. 581 (1889) at 600.

61 In *United States* v. *Pink*, 315 U.S. 203 (1942), the Supreme Court upheld an executive agreement over inconsistent state laws.

62 "*United States-Measures Affecting Alcoholic and Malt Beverages*" Report of the Panel, adopted 16 March, 1992, DS 23/R.

63 "*United States-Measures Affecting Alcoholic and Malt Beverages*" Report, para. 5.90.

domestic American case on the relationship between the NAFTA and federal law. When assessing whether the NAFTA could preempt inconsistent state law, the court stated "by virtue of the Supremacy Clause, a state law that conflicts with the NAFTA is preempted by the NAFTA"[64]. Federal powers regarding inconsistent state laws go further than preemption. It is clear that a federal law can pretermit any areas where state regulations can affect international trade[65].

(d) THE EFFECT OF THE EXTENT OF OBLIGATIONS LANGUAGE

The extent of obligation language could require national governments to enforce the Agreement against their subnational governments, regardless of the jurisdictional questions which arise. This has raised some concern in both Canada and the United States.

In Canada, there has been much speculation on the meaning of the "all necessary measures" obligation. This wording could require the Canadian federal government to pursue all legal avenues that might plausibly allow it to gain the jurisdiction necessary to enforce these provisions. This could result in significant constitutional questions being considered by the Canadian courts[66]. In the United States, this provision could lead to the federal preemption of inconsistent state law.

Regarding the obligations of NAFTA Parties, there is a relevant discussion in the *Statement of Administrative Action*, which points out that[67]:

... nothing in the NAFTA requires the federal government to take legal action against state measures that NAFTA dispute settlement panels may determine to be inconsistent with trade obligations. Under the NAFTA, panel opinions are advisory only. If the defending country loses, it is not required to remove or change the offending measure. It may offer trade compensation instead or simply permit the other country to take retaliatory action of equivalent effect.

---

64 Per Ritchie, J. in *Public Citizen et al* v. *Office of the U.S. Trade Representative*, 872 F. Supp. 21 at 33 (D.C. 1993). Overturned by the U.S. Circuit Court of Appeals for the District of Columbia, Sept, 24, 1993; awaiting appeal to the Supreme Court.

65 This point is made by Robert Sedler in "Federal and State Power over International Trade under the United States Constitution" in M. Irish and E. Carasco eds., *The Legal Framework for Canada-United States Trade* (Toronto: Carswell, 1987) at 172.

66 Other impacts could be the requirement that the federal government reactivate its long dormant power to disallow provincial legislation or its ability to reserve provincial legislation for an indefinite period. Both of these powers have not been used for almost half a century.

67 *Statement of Administrative Action* at 102. A similar, but more brief statement occurs in the *Statement of Government Action* at 78.

This statement provides some diplomatic assurances to states that the federal government may not necessarily preempt their inconsistent laws. While it is correct that Parties are not required to amend their laws based on the findings of NAFTA dispute panels, NAFTA article 105 still requires them to take all necessary measures to comply. Thus the question of the extent to which federal governments will go to exact compliance from subnational governments still remains unresolved.

3. THE RELATIONSHIP BETWEEN THE NAFTA AND OTHER AGREEMENTS

In the NAFTA, each country affirmed its rights and obligations under the GATT and other international agreements. However, article 103(2) provides that the NAFTA takes priority over all other international agreements unless otherwise stated in the NAFTA. NAFTA article 104 provides an example where other international agreements take priority over the NAFTA in the case of an inconsistency, provided that the Party chooses the alternative that is the least inconsistent with the other provisions of Agreement[68]:

(a) the *Convention on International Trade in Endangered Species of Wild Fauna and Flora*, signed at Washington, March 3, 1973, as amended June 22, 1979;

(b) the *Montreal Protocol on Substances that Deplete the Ozone Layer*, signed at Montreal, September 16, 1987, as amended June 29, 1990;

(c) the *Basel Convention on the Control of Transboundary Movements of Hazardous Wastes and Their Disposal*, done at Basel, March 22, 1989, on its entry into force for Canada, Mexico and the United States;

(d) the *Agreement Between the Government of Canada and the Government of the United States of America Concerning the Transboundary Movement of Hazardous Waste*, signed at Ottawa, October 28, 1986; and

(e) the *Agreement Between the United States of America and the United Mexican States on Cooperation for the Protection and Improvement of the Environment in the Border Area*, signed at La Paz, Baja California Sur, August 14, 1983.

---

68 Treaties take precedence "to the extent of the inconsistency, provided that where a Party has a choice among equally effective and reasonably available means of complying with such obligations, the Party chooses the alternative that is the least inconsistent with the other provisions of this Agreement".

In addition, the NAFTA allows its Parties to agree to modify the list of environmental and conservation agreements which take precedence over the NAFTA[69]. For example, in an exchange of letters by the three Parties, the *Convention on the Protection of Migratory Birds between Canada and the United States* and the *Convention for the Protection of Migratory Birds and Game Mammals between the United States and Mexico* were added to the list[70].

4. THE RELATIONSHIP BETWEEN THE NAFTA AND THE CANADA-U.S. FREE TRADE AGREEMENT

Much of the NAFTA was based on the framework of the Canada-U.S. Free Trade Agreement. By agreement between the two countries, the provisions of the Canada-U.S. Free Trade Agreement, other than those sections incorporated into NAFTA chapters, have been suspended during the time that the NAFTA is in force[71].

5. THE RELATIONSHIP BETWEEN THE NAFTA AND THE GATT

The NAFTA negotiators took significant pains to establish some form of consistency between the NAFTA and the General Agreement of Tariffs and Trade. As a result, the NAFTA incorporates directly, or by reference, a number of GATT obligations. In addition, a number of its chapters roughly mirror sections of the Tokyo Round or Uruguay Round GATT[72]. Finally, a large number of terms in the NAFTA appear to be based on definitions which have been developed by "GATT jurisprudence"[73]. Thus, the interpretative and substantive analysis of earlier GATT panel decisions may have some significant impact on the NAFTA. Whatever the apparent consistency in approach and substance between the NAFTA and the GATT,

---

69 NAFTA article 104(2).
70 The *Statement of Government Action* refers to an Exchange of Letters dated Oct. 13, 1993 between the Parties agreeing to modify annex 104.1 at 77.
71 This was accomplished through the American implementing legislation in §107 of the *North American Free Trade Implementation Act*. In Canada, there was no similar provision in the Canadian implementing legislation, but the *Statement of Government Action* claims that both Canada and the United States have agreed to suspend that agreement through a future agreement at 77.
72 In particular, the provisions on services are highly similar to the General Agreement on Tariffs and Trade, and the NAFTA intellectual property provisions in chapter 17 were highly influenced by the draft Uruguay Round GATT chapter on intellectual property.
73 For example, obligations on national treatment, Most-Favoured-Nation treatment or the GATT's general exceptions in GATT Article XX.

NAFTA article 103(2) makes clear that NAFTA provisions will take priority over inconsistent provisions in other agreements.

Another relationship between the NAFTA and the GATT can be seen by the role that the North American trading zone has under GATT rules. NAFTA article 101 establishes a free trade area between Canada, Mexico and the United States, consistent with Article XXIV of the GATT. This statement however is not conclusive proof that the NAFTA is GATT-consistent. When Canada and the United States entered into the Autopact Agreement in 1965[74], the United States applied to the GATT Council to obtain a waiver from the obligations of GATT Article XXIV[75]. No waiver was requested by either Canada or the United States for the Canada-U.S. Free Trade Agreement, but both governments notified the GATT Council[76] of the Agreement. Similarly, the government of Canada has notified the GATT Council of the NAFTA[77].

---

74 *Agreement Concerning Automotive Products Between the Government of Canada and the Government of the United States of America.* C.T.S. 1966. no. 14., [1966] 1 U.S.T. 1372.
75 The GATT decision was taken on Dec. 20, 1965. United States - Imports of Automotive Products, GATT, BISD, 14 Supp. 37 (1966).
76 Pursuant to GATT Article XXIV:7 notification occurred on Jan. 27, 1989 (GATT L/6464). Both countries made a submission to the GATT Council on Oct. 27, 1989 (GATT L/6464 at 1).
77 The date of notification was Jan. 24, 1994.

3

National Treatment and Market Access in Goods

1. MARKET ACCESS

Market access provisions are the "meat and potatoes" of traditional trade agreements. These provisions detail tariff and market access concessions for goods which qualify as originating in a Party to the agreement. The NAFTA attempts to enhance access to markets for goods produced and traded within North America. Increasing access to markets was a significant negotiating goal for the American government. The Administration made this clear during the Congressional NAFTA debate where it stated[1]:

> Export growth has been by far the most dynamic part of the U.S. economy in recent years, and continuous efforts to open new markets must guide our strategy to secure new growth and create new jobs. . . . The NAFTA's first and most basic achievement is to remove the vast majority of barriers which distort trade among the United States and two of its largest trading partners. By the end of the transition period, the Canadian and Mexican markets will be open permanently to the products of U.S. workers. U.S. firms and workers will be able to compete on an equal basis with Mexican and Canadian firms on their own turf. And U.S. firms will have an advantage over Japanese and European firms, whose products will still be subject to all Mexican and some Canadian tariffs.

The NAFTA Market Access chapter establishes the basic national treatment obligation of the Parties. It also contains rules regarding tariff elimination, quantitative restrictions such as quotas, licenses and permits, and import and export price requirements. While this NAFTA chapter provides for special treatment for the automotive and textile sectors, these will be assessed in the next chapter of this book dealing with the NAFTA Rules of Origin chapter.

---

1 *Statement as to How the NAFTA Serves the Interest of United States Commerce,* appended to the *Statement of Administrative Action* at 1.

(a) NATIONAL TREATMENT

The NAFTA incorporates the same national treatment obligation as contained in Article III of the GATT[2]. This article establishes a number of important obligations upon the GATT Parties. The GATT rules recognize that internal taxes and charges, measures affecting the treatment of goods and internal quantitative regulations, will not be applied in a way that gives protection to domestic production[3]. Imported products from a GATT Party will not be subject, directly or indirectly, to internal taxes or other charges unless those same charges are applied to similar domestic products[4]. These same products must be given treatment no less favourable than that given to similar domestic products in respect of all laws, regulations and requirements affecting their internal sale[5]. The GATT Article III national treatment provision does not apply to government procurement[6] nor to domestic subsidies[7].

Under the NAFTA, the national treatment obligation extends to the measures of state and provincial governments unless that government has made a reservation to the particular NAFTA obligation[8]. Subnational governments are required to provide the best treatment to the goods of another NAFTA Party that they provide to the goods of any other domestic subnational government[9].

Cases decided by GATT panels regarding the meaning of the national treatment obligation may have a significant influence on how the NAFTA national treatment obligation is interpreted. Recent GATT panels have determined that the granting of formally equal treatment to domestic and foreign products may not satisfy the national treatment obligation. What must be provided is "effective equality of opportunities for imported products"[10].

Each NAFTA Party has set out a detailed list of exceptions to the national treatment obligation for goods in annex 301.3. As well, NAFTA Parties are entitled to rely on whatever reservations to national treatment that they made in their Protocol of Provisional Application when they first became GATT Parties. Canada and the United States were both original members of the GATT. Their exemptions under the Protocol of Provisional

---

2 NAFTA article 301.
3 GATT Article III:1.
4 GATT Article III:1.
5 GATT Article III:1.
6 GATT Article III:8(a).
7 GATT Article III:8(b).
8 The issue of reservations is covered in this book more fully in chapter 21.
9 NAFTA article 301(2).
10 GATT panel decision on s. 337 of the U.S. *Tariff Act of 1930* (adopted on Nov. 7, 1989, GATT L/6439) at 51.

Application relate to measures which they have continually maintained since October 30, 1947. Mexico only recently joined the GATT. It is entitled to maintain otherwise-inconsistent measures based on its Protocol's entry into force of August 24, 1986[11].

(b) TARIFF ELIMINATION

All goods that meet the NAFTA rules of origin will have their tariffs eliminated. No new tariffs may be imposed on goods from a NAFTA Party[12]. Tariff elimination is scheduled in four staging categories. Category A goods became duty free when the NAFTA came into force[13]. Other categories will become duty free as follows:

Category B	January 1, 1998
Category C	January 1, 2003
Category C+	January 1, 2008

Tariff elimination under the Canada-U.S. Free Trade Agreement will continue as scheduled under that agreement[14]. For certain items, tariffs will be phased out over a period of up to 15 years. Tariff cuts will be based on the tariff rates in effect on July 1, 1991. As in the Canada-U.S. Free Trade Agreement, the NAFTA allows its Parties to agree to accelerate tariff phase-outs.

In order to enjoy the benefit of the North American free trade zone, goods must comply with the NAFTA rules of origin. These content rules specify that goods originate in North America if they are wholly North American. Goods containing non-regional materials are considered to be North American if the non-regional materials are sufficiently transformed in the NAFTA region. In some cases, goods must include a specified percentage of North American content.

(c) DUTY DRAWBACKS

Duty drawbacks refer to the refunding of customs duties paid when a good imported into a NAFTA country is incorporated into a good exported to another Party. Manufacturers will be able to collect a refund equal to the lesser of the duties paid on imported inputs, or the duties assessed on exports of finished products[15]. The NAFTA provides for duty drawbacks

---

11 GATT, BISD, 33 Supp. 3.
12 NAFTA article 302.
13 NAFTA annex 302.2(1).
14 This is provided for in NAFTA annex 302.2(4).
15 NAFTA article 303(3).

on Canadian and American goods until January 1, 1996 and until January 1, 2001 on trade between Canada or the United States and Mexico[16]. The duty drawback provisions do not apply to goods which are shipped-in-bond[17] or to goods for which there has been no change in condition from when they were imported, for example goods which were only cleaned, packed or tested in a Party[18]. Annex 303.6 contains exceptions to the duty drawback rules for citrus products, products under the U.S. sugar re-export program, duties paid on textiles imported and made into exported apparel[19], and television sets[20].

The NAFTA also prohibits the use of duty waivers or duty remissions which are tied to specific performance requirements[21]. Mexico has agreed to change its domestic law to allow products made in the Maquiladoras to be sold into its national market.

(d) IMPORT AND EXPORT RESTRICTIONS

The NAFTA prohibits the use of import and export restrictions except in accordance with GATT Article XI[22]. This GATT article, which is incorporated into the NAFTA[23], prohibits export and import prohibitions except for certain public policy reasons such as dealing with critical shortages of foodstuffs or the grading of goods. The restrictions which are prohibited include not only bans, but also export price requirements[24].

The NAFTA permits existing quantitative restrictions to be maintained if they are listed in annex 301.3. This annex allows Canada to impose certain export restrictions on such goods as logs and unprocessed fish[25]. The NAFTA also prohibits the introduction of new customs users fees on NAFTA Parties[26]. This same annex allows the United States to impose controls on the exports of logs as well as maintain its restrictive shipping provisions in the *Jones Act*. Mexico is also permitted to impose similar measures.

---

16 NAFTA annex 303.6.
17 NAFTA article 303(6)(a).
18 NAFTA article 303(6)(b).
19 NAFTA annex 303.6.
20 NAFTA annex 303.8.
21 NAFTA articles 304-307.
22 NAFTA article 309.
23 NAFTA article 309(1) incorporates this article, its interpretive notes and any successor article into the NAFTA.
24 NAFTA article 309(2).
25 This is the same as contained in article 1203 of the Canada-U.S. Free Trade Agreement. These export exceptions may be important within the debate on whether unbottled fresh water is covered by the NAFTA. This question is discussed in some detail later in this book.
26 NAFTA article 310.

(e) GOODS USED FOR TEMPORARY ENTRANTS

The NAFTA requires temporary duty-free status to certain goods used to assist business persons[27] who qualify for temporary entry under NAFTA's chapter 16 rules. These goods include:

- professional equipment needed by a business person who qualifies for temporary entry in NAFTA chapter 16;
- equipment for print or broadcast media;
- goods for sports purposes; and
- commercial samples and advertising film.

Persons who are granted this temporary duty-free status may not sell these items within the territory that they are temporarily in.

(f) EXPORT TAXES AND OTHER MEASURES

The NAFTA restricts Parties from imposing export taxes on goods unless that Party also imposes a similar charge on goods sold in its domestic market[28]. This charge must also be assessed against the good irrespective of whether the good is foreign or domestic. Mexico has been permitted to maintain a number of otherwise-inconsistent taxes regarding domestic foodstuffs[29].

If a Party takes an export measure for the purposes of the conservation of exhaustible natural resources, to ensure essential quantities of a good for domestic price stabilization or to preserve foodstuffs during times of critical shortage[30], then the NAFTA imposes a proportional sharing obligation[31]. For a NAFTA Party to rely on these reasons to reduce the supply of a good it must abide by the following[32]:

(a) proportional access of the good must be made available to the other Party on the basis of the average supply over the last 36-month period;

(b) a Party may not impose a higher price for exports than the price charged domestically by way of taxes, royalties or minimum price regulations; and

---

27 NAFTA article 305.
28 NAFTA article 314.
29 NAFTA annex 314.
30 These are measures which are justified under the GATT exceptions XX(g),(i) or (j).
31 NAFTA article 315.
32 NAFTA article 315.

(c) the restriction does not require the disruption of normal channels of supply of that good.

This article only places obligations on the governments of Canada and the United States and does not apply to Mexico[33].

(g) COUNTRY OF ORIGIN MARKINGS

The NAFTA requires that its Parties create rules for the marking of country of origin on goods[34]. Products must have clear, conspicuous and permanent origin marks.

(h) WINE AND DISTILLED SPIRITS

The NAFTA prohibits the imposition of measures which require the blending of distilled spirits imported from another Party with local spirits[35]. The Agreement incorporates the provisions of the Canada-U.S. Free Trade Agreement regarding the listing, sale and distribution of wine and distilled spirits between Canada and the United States[36]. Provisions regarding trade between Canada and Mexico are also set out[37]. The NAFTA Parties agree to recognize that certain distinctive spirits can only come from designated areas. These products are, for the United States: Bourbon Whiskey and Tennessee Whiskey; for Canada: Canadian Whiskey; and for Mexico: Tequila and Mezcal[38].

(i) CONSULTATIONS

The NAFTA creates a Committee on Trade in Goods which will deal with all matters arising from the Trade in Goods chapter[39]. In addition, Parties are required to hold a meeting each year to discuss the operation of the NAFTA with their own customs, immigration, food and agriculture inspection, and border inspection officials.

---

33 NAFTA annex 315.
34 NAFTA article 311.
35 NAFTA article 312.
36 NAFTA annex 312.2, Section A.
37 NAFTA annex 312.2, Section B.
38 NAFTA annex 313.
39 NAFTA article 316.

4

Rules of Origin

Like all trade agreements, the NAFTA takes considerable effort to define what constitutes a good originating from a NAFTA country. The goal of the rule of origin provisions is to increase the amount of certainty and predicability in the three-way NAFTA Party trade. The rules of origin were carefully designed to ensure that the beneficial NAFTA tariffs are accessed by enterprises that produce goods in the NAFTA market.

1. GENERAL RULES

Goods which qualify as being from the NAFTA Parties will be able to qualify for NAFTA tariff treatment[1]. The basic NAFTA rule of origin provides that goods originate in North America if they are wholly obtained or produced in North America[2]. Goods containing non-North American content will qualify if they change tariff classification by being substantially transformed within a NAFTA Party into another good. For example, such a substantial transformation occurs when raw logs are processed into plywood sheeting. In certain circumstances, goods must include a specified percentage of North American content in addition to meeting the tariff classification requirement.

The NAFTA rules of origin will also allow goods to be treated as NAFTA-originating when the finished good is specifically named in the same tariff subheading as its parts and it meets the required regional value content test[3]. There are two methods of assessing regional value content: the "transaction-value" and the "net-cost" method[4].

The "net-cost" method requires that ineligible costs be deducted from the total cost of producing the product. Examples of excluded costs are sales promotions, royalties, marketing, after-sales costs and certain interest amounts[5]. This results in the net-cost. The value of any non-NAFTA

---

1 NAFTA article 302.
2 NAFTA article 401. This is defined in NAFTA article 415 to include goods which were extracted, caught or bred in the territory of the Party.
3 NAFTA article 401(d).
4 NAFTA article 402(1).
5 NAFTA article 402(3).

originating materials are then deducted and this amount is divided by the net cost. This provides the regional value content.

In the transaction value method, the value of all non-originating materials is deducted from the transaction value of the good. This amount is divided by the transaction value to arrive at the regional value content[6]. For a good to qualify under the NAFTA, it must contain at least 60 percent NAFTA content.

Since the transaction value method involves higher values than the net cost method, the NAFTA requires a higher regional content value under the transaction value method. It is estimated that the transaction value method may increase the North American value content by one to two percent over the net cost method[7]. While both methods are available to industry, the "net-cost" method is prescribed when the "transaction-value" method is not acceptable under the GATT Customs Valuation Code or for certain products, such as automotive goods, footwear or sales between related enterprises[8]. This marks a change from the Canada-U.S. Free Trade Agreement where only transaction value was permitted to calculate regional value content[9]. The regional value rules also will dispense with the contentious Canadian-American issue over the interpretation of the appropriate value of regional content to apply to a Japanese-Canadian joint venture automotive plant[10].

2. AUTOMOTIVE TRADE

The NAFTA treats automotive trade not in one trilateral agreement but in two bilateral understandings. This treatment is on account of the highly developed automotive trade arrangements between Canada and the United States. Because of the impact of the Canada-U.S. Autopact[11] and the Canada-U.S. Free Trade Agreement, most automotive trade between these two countries already is duty-free. The NAFTA maintains the Autopact in force between Canada and the United States[12].

---

6 NAFTA article 402(2).
7 Frédéric Cantin & Andreas Lowenfeld. "Rules of Origin, the Canada-U.S. FTA and the Honda Case" 87 *American Journal of International Law*, 375 (July 1993) at 387.
8 NAFTA article 402(5).
9 Section XVII of Canada-U.S. Free Trade Agreement Annex 301.2.
10 NAFTA annex 403.3.
11 *Agreement concerning Automotive Products between the Government of Canada and the Government of the United States of America*, signed at Johnson City, Texas, Jan. 16, 1965.
12 NAFTA Appendix 300-A.1(1).

Regarding Mexico, the United States agreed to:

- eliminate tariffs on passenger vehicles;
- reduce tariffs on light trucks to 10 percent and then phase them out over the next five years; and
- phase out tariffs on other vehicles over the next 10 years.

For imports from Canada and the United States, Mexico will reduce its tariffs on passenger vehicles and light trucks. Passenger vehicles will have a 10-year tariff phase-out while the phase-out for light trucks will be five years. All tariffs on other vehicles will be phased-out by January 1, 2003. Canada has agreed to end its tariffs on automotive goods imported from Mexico over time.

(a) RULES OF ORIGIN

The NAFTA changed the percentage of North American content re-quired from the Canada-U.S. Free Trade Agreement. The earlier agreement required that there be 50 percent North American content in order to qualify for preferred treatment. The NAFTA rules of origin will be increased over time on the following basis[13].

Year	Percentage of North American Content	
	Passenger automobiles, light trucks, engines and some transmissions	Other Parts
1994	50%	50%
1998	56%	55%
2004	62.5%	60%

In calculating the content level of automotive goods, the value of imports of automotive parts from outside the NAFTA region will be traced through the production chain[14]. This eliminates the "roll-up" rule in the Canada-U.S. Free Trade Agreement that allowed a component which had 50 percent regional value, and thus qualified as an originating good, to have its full value counted towards the calculation of regional value for the

---

13 NAFTA article 403(5).
14 NAFTA article 404(1).

product that incorporates it. It should be noted that the NAFTA permits automobile producers to use regional content averaging.

NAFTA article 405 provides for a *de minimis* exception to prevent goods from losing NAFTA status because of a minimal amount of non-NAFTA content. Under this rule, NAFTA provides that a small amount of non-North American content will not change the determination of a good from being treated as being a NAFTA regional good. This minimal value is capped at not more than seven percent of the transaction value of the good on an F.O.B. basis[15].

(b) CAFE RULES

NAFTA provides that the United States will amend its Corporate Average Fuel Economy (CAFE) rules, to allow Mexican-manufactured parts and vehicles to be classified as domestic[16]. After a 10-year period, Mexican production exported to the United States will be treated the same as U.S. or Canadian production[17]. The NAFTA does not change the treatment of Canadian-manufactured vehicles which already qualify under these CAFE rules.

(c) MEXICAN AUTO DECREE

The NAFTA requires Mexico to eliminate its domestic automotive investment and trade regime (the Auto Decree[18] and the Autotransportation Decree[19]) over 10 years[20]. North American producers of passenger vehicles[21] (that is, those that already have production in Mexico) and of trucks and buses gain immediate access to the Mexican market. North American producers who do not now make cars in Mexico, including transplants, will not be able to export to Mexico until after the 10-year transition period. During this time, the Mexican government has agreed to change this law to

---

15 NAFTA article 405(1). F.O.B. means Free on Board. It describes a point, in the direct shipment of goods from seller to buyer, when the goods have been physically transmitted onto a transportation method.

16 NAFTA Appendix 300-A-A.3(1).

17 The Labor Advisory Committee on the NAFTA, a body established under the U.S. *Trade Act of 1974* to advise the U.S. Trade Representative and Congress, has suggested that the inclusion of Mexican vehicles into the domestic CAFE calculation will allow a concentration of small car production by the "Big Three" American auto producers in Mexico. *Preliminary Report*, Labor Advisory Committee, Sept. 16, 1992 at 9.

18 *Decreto para el Fomento y Modernizacion de la Industria Automotriz* (1989).

19 *Decreto para el Fomento y Modernizacion de la Industria Manufacturera de Vehiculos de Autotransporte* (1989).

20 NAFTA Appendix 300-A.2(1).

21 General Motors, Ford, Chrysler, Volkswagen and Nissan would qualify under this basis.

end trade balancing that linked vehicle imports to Mexican vehicle sales[22]. Mexico will modify its performance requirements to allow vehicle assemblers to reduce the level of part and vehicle exports required to import such goods[23].

In the NAFTA, Mexico has committed to modify its "national value-added" rules by reducing the percentage of parts required to be purchased from Mexican producers[24]. This will be accomplished by counting purchases from maquiladoras towards this percentage[25]. Canadian, Mexican and American parts manufacturers may participate in the Mexican market during the transition period, while parts assemblers in Mexico will be required to purchase parts from Mexican producers. At the end of the transition period, the value added requirement will be eliminated.

(d) IMPORTS OF USED VEHICLES

The Canada-U.S. Free Trade Agreement ended Canadian restrictions on used vehicles imports from the United States on January 1, 1994. Beginning in January 1, 2009, Canada will phase out its prohibition on imports of Mexican used vehicles over 10 years. Mexico will phase out its prohibition on imports of Canadian and American cars on a reciprocal basis.

3. TEXTILES AND APPAREL GOODS

The NAFTA provides a separate set of rules for trade in textile and apparel goods. The Agreement provides for a 10-year tariff phase-out for most apparel products and eight years for most textile products[26]. Tariffs on NAFTA-originating textiles and apparel will follow the tariff provisions of the Canada-U.S. Free Trade Agreement which will make that market duty free by January 1, 1998.

The NAFTA creates a special rule of origin requirement for textiles and apparel which is known as the "yarn-forward rule". This rule requires North American content in the yarn, from its production to its incorporation into an apparel product. To qualify, these goods must pass a "triple transformation test". This requires that the good be cut and sewn from fabric made from North American fibres in a NAFTA Party.

This rule is one step stricter than the "double transformation test" required under the Canada-U.S. Free Trade Agreement for its preferential

---

22 NAFTA annex 602.3(17).
23 NAFTA annex 602.3(12).
24 NAFTA annex 602.3(5).
25 NAFTA annex 602.3(4).
26 NAFTA annex 300-B, s. 2.

treatment. Under the "double transformation test," foreign fabric could be given preferential treatment if it was cut and sewn in either Canada or the United States into a finished product.

There are a small number of fabrics which are exempt from the "triple transformation test" under the NAFTA. In addition, yarn, fabric and apparel that do not qualify under the NAFTA test may still qualify for NAFTA treatment if they can be allocated into a tariff preference level (TPL)[27]. Each TPL is permanent and has a growth factor, unlike the tariff rate quotas established under the Canada-U.S. Free Trade Agreement.

The NAFTA allows a Party to take safeguard actions during the period of tariff phase-out if the impact of textile and apparel goods imports from another NAFTA Party caused "serious damage or actual threat thereof"[28]. As well, the Agreement provides that refunds of duties paid on imported components of goods which have then been exported (duty drawback), will be extended for two years beyond the expiry of the same program in the Canada-U.S. Free Trade Agreement. In 1996, duty drawback will be replaced with a permanent duty refund system.

The NAFTA Parties have agreed to review the rule of origin provisions of the Agreement within the first five years of the NAFTA's operation[29].

---

27 NAFTA annex 300-B, Appendix 6(B).
28 NAFTA annex 300-B, s. 4.
29 NAFTA annex 300-B, s. 7.2.

5

Customs Administration

Under the Canada-U.S. Free Trade Agreement, customs administration rules became the subject of some dispute[1]. This is not surprising given the extent of bilateral Canadian-American trade. Bilateral trade flows between these countries in 1992 totalled $267.5 billion[2]. With this great amount of trade, it became essential that the NAFTA improve upon the earlier bilateral agreement. The NAFTA customs administration procedures mark an improvement over the shorter provisions contained in the Canada-U.S. Free Trade Agreement Annex 406.

1. CERTIFICATE OF ORIGIN

The NAFTA Customs Administration chapter requires the Parties to develop a common certificate of origin and sets out procedures for the certificate[3]. Certificates are required for all goods in excess of US $1,000[4]. Exporters, not producers, are responsible for having a valid certificate[5]. Importers must have a certificate for all goods upon which they want to claim NAFTA treatment[6]. Certificates can cover one importation or multiple importations of the same good for a one-year period. They remain valid for four years from their date of signature.

The NAFTA includes a provision dealing with goods which are eligible for preferential NAFTA treatment, but for which the preferential treatment was not claimed. In this circumstance, the importer may claim a refund of duties for up to one year[7]. This marks a change in American practice which generally only allowed for a 90-day period to claim excess-contributions[8].

---

1 An example is the U.S. dispute regarding the interpretation of s. 304 of the Canada-U.S. Free Trade Agreement.
2 Figures are in Canadian dollars. Source: Statistics Canada, Cat. No. 67-001.
3 NAFTA article 501.
4 NAFTA article 501(4). Although transporters may be required to provide invoices to national authorities to prove that the goods are of North American origin.
5 NAFTA article 510(4).
6 NAFTA article 502(2)(a).
7 NAFTA article 502(3).
8 19 U.S.C. §1504 (1988).

2. RECORD KEEPING AND VERIFICATION

The NAFTA imposes a common five-year record-keeping requirement on exporters and producers for traded goods[9]. It also allows national customs authorities to conduct verifications of regional value. These verifications will be based upon visits to the producer's or exporter's premises and written questionnaires. Verification of regional value content will be based on the General Accepted Accounting Practices in the exporter's country[10]. This will prevent disputes arising between the Parties from differences in national accounting practices.

3. ADVANCE RULINGS

An important addition in the NAFTA is the introduction of procedures to allow for consistent interpretation, application and administration of the rules of origin between its Parties[11]. The NAFTA allows importers, exporters and producers to obtain from any NAFTA customs authority advance rulings on how it would treat certain goods[12]. If the ruling is unfavourable, the customs authority must provide full reasons for the ruling[13]. Similar material facts and circumstances require the customs authorities to provide similar rulings[14]. While the position taken by a customs authority in an advance ruling can be modified, if an exporter relies on an advance ruling, the Party must delay any modification for up to 90 days[15]. Exporters and producers from other NAFTA Parties have substantially the same rights of review and appeal as domestic importers of rulings pertaining to origin and advance rulings[16].

4. CONSULTATIONS

To continue the ongoing consultative process on customs administration, NAFTA article 513 creates a NAFTA Party Working Group on Rules of Origin to deal with:

---

9 NAFTA article 505. Records must be kept for five years.
10 NAFTA article 506(8). This clause remedies the earlier Canadian-American dispute on the calculation of regional value content.
11 NAFTA article 511.
12 NAFTA article 509. This creates a new process for Canadian and Mexican customs authorities.
13 NAFTA article 509(3)(c).
14 NAFTA article 509(5).
15 NAFTA article 509(8).
16 NAFTA article 510.

- implementation of article 303 on duty drawback and deferral;
- Most-Favoured Nation rates on certain goods (article 308);
- origin markings (article 311);
- the rules of origin (chapter 4);
- the chapter on customs administration (chapter 5);
- marking rules and uniform regulations; and
- the effective administration of customs-related aspects of the Market Access chapter (chapter 3).

This working group must meet at least four times annually and on the request of any NAFTA Party to provide a means of avoiding lengthy disputes over customs administration issues.

6
Energy

Provisions on energy were a sensitive topic for all NAFTA Parties. American negotiators wished to succeed in their long-held desire to obtain secure access to Mexican energy resources. Maintaining national control of the oil industry is so deeply rooted in the Mexican national identity that its constitution specifically prohibits foreign ownership in the petroleum industry[1]. Finally, while Canada and the United States had an energy agreement in their earlier Free Trade Agreement, there was political sensitivity over scarcity of supply issues. These tensions led to a NAFTA chapter which could not conceivably live up to the expectations of all Parties. Thus, it is not surprising to find that the NAFTA negotiators were unable to achieve a comprehensive agreement over energy.

1. SCOPE

The NAFTA Energy chapter applies to measures relating to crude oil, gas, refined products, basic petrochemicals, coal, electricity and nuclear energy and measures relating to investment and services associated with energy goods[2]. Mexico has reserved a number of strategic areas from the application of this chapter[3]. These include:[4]

(a) exploration, exploitation and refining of crude oil and natural gas;
(b) foreign trade, storage and distribution of crude oil, natural and artificial gas, refined oil and natural gas and basic petrochemicals;
(c) supply of electricity as a public service; and
(d) exploration, exploitation and processing of radioactive materials.

Private investment is not permitted in any of these areas, nor are service contracts allowed, without the permission of the Mexican government[5].

---

1 Article 27, para. 4 of the Mexican Constitution of 1917.
2 NAFTA article 602.
3 The Mexican Constitition prohibits foreign ownership in these strategic areas. Mexican Constitution, article 28, para. 4 and article 25.
4 NAFTA annex 602.3(1).
5 NAFTA annex 602.3(2).

In addition, Mexico will allow enterprises of NAFTA Parties to establish, acquire and operate electrical generating facilities in Mexico to meet that enterprise's supply needs[6]. Independent electricity generation and co-generation facilities will also be permitted, however excess energy from these facilities must be sold to CFE, the Mexican electricity utility.

On account of the constitutional concerns from Mexico, the NAFTA Parties made specific mention of their full respect for their constitutions[7] and their desire to increase trade in energy[8].

2. OBLIGATIONS

The NAFTA establishes a number of obligations upon its Parties regarding the treatment and supply of energy.

(a) IMPORT AND EXPORT RESTRICTIONS

The NAFTA incorporates the GATT provisions which deal with the prohibition or restriction on trade in energy and basic petrochemical goods[9] to the extent that they do not conflict with other provisions in the Energy chapter[10]. The incorporation of these obligations requires NAFTA Parties to not impose minimum or maximum export price requirements or import price requirements except to the extent necessary to enforce countervailing or antidumping duty orders[11]. The GATT Protocols of Provisional Application have not been incorporated into this NAFTA obligation.

Parties may adopt or maintain restrictions on energy imports or exports from non-Parties. If a Party imposes a restriction on a non-Party, the other NAFTA Parties will avoid undue interference with it[12]. Each Party may administer export and import licensing systems for energy and basic petrochemical goods, provided that they are operated in a manner consistent with the Agreement[13]. Mexico has reserved the right to restrict the granting of licenses for a number of petrochemical goods[14].

---

6 NAFTA annex 602.3(5).

7 NAFTA article 601.

8 Presumably, the NAFTA negotiators included this reference to national constitutions to assuage Mexican concerns regarding their energy restrictions in their constitution. It is important to note that this reference is not limited to the Energy chapter and could be used to assist NAFTA panels when dealing with extent of obligation issues regarding subnational governments.

9 Such as GATT Article XI.

10 NAFTA article 603(1).

11 NAFTA article 603(2).

12 NAFTA article 603(3).

13 NAFTA article 603(5).

14 NAFTA annex 603.6.

(b) EXPORT TAXES AND OTHER EXPORT MEASURES

The NAFTA prohibits the imposition of a tax, duty or charge on the export of energy or basic petrochemical goods unless the same measure is applied domestically and to all exports[15]. The NAFTA imposes significant limits on the ability of governments to impose import and export restrictions. Limits can only be imposed to address matters such as:

- preventing or relieving critical shortages on a temporary basis[16];
- conserving exhaustible natural resources[17];
- ensuring essential supplies for domestic industries as part of a domestic government stabilization plan[18]; or
- dealing with matters essential to the acquisition or distribution of products in short supply[19].

For a NAFTA Party to rely on these reasons to reduce the supply of energy it must abide by the following[20]:

(a) proportional access of the good must be made available to the other Party on the basis of the average supply over the last 36-month period;

(b) a Party may not impose a higher price for exports than the price charged domestically by way of taxes, royalties or minimum price regulation; and

(c) the restriction does not require the disruption of normal channels of supply of that good.

The NAFTA replicates the wording of article 904 of the Canada-U.S. Free Trade Agreement and also incorporates it into the NAFTA[21]. NAFTA article 608(2) incorporates Canada-U.S. Free Trade Agreement annex 902.5 and 905.2 which establishes the primacy of the *International Energy Program* over the NAFTA in the case of any inconsistency between them regarding the obligation of proportionality.

Canada and the United States are members of the International Energy Program. Parties to the International Energy Program[22] undertake similar energy sharing obligations as under the NAFTA. There are several key differences based on the nature of the two agreements. For example, the

---

15 NAFTA article 604.
16 GATT Article XI:2(a).
17 GATT Article XX(g).
18 GATT Article XX(i).
19 GATT Article XX(j).
20 NAFTA article 605.
21 NAFTA annex 608.2.
22 *Agreement on an International Energy Program*, T.I.A.S. No. 8278 (1976).

International Energy Program covers emergency shortages in oil only while the NAFTA deals with scarcity in all forms of energy. In addition the International Energy Program establishes a general sharing obligation, while the NAFTA imposes sharing based on the preceding 36-months' production.

The government of Canada issued a statement on the NAFTA energy provisions on December 3, 1993. The statement provided that:[23]

> In the event of shortage or in order to conserve Canada's exhaustible energy resources, the Government will interpret and apply the NAFTA in a way which maximizes energy security for Canadians. The Government interprets the NAFTA as not requiring any Canadian to export a given level or proportion of any energy resource to another NAFTA country.

This view differs from the American government. In a letter to Representative Edward Markey, President Clinton set out the administration's view on this issue. He wrote that the U.S. government would accept no change to the proportionality commitment contained in the NAFTA[24]. The proportionality requirements bind only governments. There is no limitation on private market actors bidding up the price of the oil and thereby keeping it in Canada[25].

3. ENERGY REGULATORY MEASURES

The NAFTA includes provisions on energy regulatory measures. It establishes an obligation on energy regulatory bodies to apply measures consistent with the NAFTA's obligation on national treatment, import and export restrictions and export taxes[26]. In addition, the Parties agreed that in the application of energy regulatory measures, governments should seek to avoid disruption of contractual relationships[27]. The scope of this section applies to national governments and subnationals that regulate energy measures.

4. NATIONAL SECURITY

The NAFTA reduces the ability of governments to use the NAFTA national security exception for energy issues. NAFTA article 607 provides

---

23 This statement is also reproduced in the *Statement of Government Action* at 119.
24 Letter of President Clinton to Representative Edward Markey (D-Mass.) Nov. 13, 1993.
25 This point is made by G.C. Watkins in "NAFTA and Energy: A Bridge Not Far Enough" in Globerman & Walker eds, *Assessing NAFTA: A Trinational Analysis.* (Vancouver: The Fraser Institute, 1993) at 208.
26 NAFTA article 606(1).
27 NAFTA article 606(2).

a special definition for national security in the context of the Energy chapter. It will allow a Party to maintain a measure restricting imports of energy or exports to the extent necessary to:

(a) supply a military establishment of a Party or enable fulfilment of a critical defense contract of a Party;

(b) respond to a situation of armed conflict involving the Party taking the measure;

(c) implement national policies or international agreements relating to the non-proliferation of nuclear weapons or other nuclear explosive devices; or

(d) respond to direct threats of disruption in the supply of nuclear materials for defense purposes.

This definition provides fewer exclusions than the general national security definition in article 2102. The Mexican government avoided commitments on proportional sharing in the NAFTA[28]. In addition, the narrow national security definition does not apply to Mexico[29].

---

28 NAFTA annex 605.
29 NAFTA annex 607.

7
Agriculture

Of the 22 NAFTA chapters, only the NAFTA Agriculture chapter does not contain a common text for the three NAFTA Parties. This chapter establishes two agreements, one on Mexican-American agricultural trade, the other on Mexican-Canadian agricultural trade. Issues of bilateral Canadian-American agricultural trade are not individually addressed by the NAFTA.

The Agriculture chapter also contains a sub-chapter dealing with restrictions on government measures on the development, adoption and enforcement of health and sanitary measures. The NAFTA also provides a special import safeguard to deal with import surges of agricultural products.

A. AGRICULTURE

1. COMMON COMMITMENTS FOR ALL PARTIES

The NAFTA sets out several common obligations on all its parties in the area of agricultural products.

(a) AGRICULTURAL SAFEGUARDS

Given the sensitivity of agricultural concerns of all NAFTA Parties, the Agreement provides for a process by which its obligations can be suspended in certain situations. During the first 10 years of the NAFTA's operation, a special safeguard provision applies to certain agricultural products. A NAFTA Party may use a safeguard if imports of products from another NAFTA Party reach a threshold amount specified in the NAFTA. In such circumstances, the importing country may snapback to the tariff rate in place when the Agreement went into effect or the prevailing Most-Favoured-Nation rate, whichever is lower[1]. The trigger levels will increase over this 10-year period.

---

1 NAFTA article 703(3). This is known as a tariff "snap back".

(b) DOMESTIC SUPPORT

The NAFTA Parties have recognized the importance of domestic support measures to their agricultural sectors and appreciate that they may have trade-distorting effects. As a result, each NAFTA Party will endeavour to move toward domestic support policies that have minimal trade-distorting effects[2]. Domestic support policies may still be modified as long as such new policies are consistent with the GATT[3].

(c) EXPORT SUBSIDIES

The NAFTA Parties have recognized that export subsidies for agricultural goods may disrupt the markets of importing countries. Through the Agreement, they have affirmed that it is inappropriate to provide export subsidies for agricultural goods sold into other NAFTA Parties, unless that Party also subsidizes that same good[4]. At the same time, Parties have maintained their rights to apply countervailing duties to subsidized imports[5].

The NAFTA requires an exporting Party to deliver three days advance notice of introduction of an export subsidy on a good exported into that Party. The Parties are required to consult on this issue within 72 hours of receiving the notice[6].

(d) COMMITTEE ON AGRICULTURAL TRADE

The NAFTA creates a Committee on Agricultural Trade to monitor the implementation and administration of the agricultural's provisions and to provide a forum for consultations on agricultural issues[7]. In addition, the following working groups will be created to assist the committee:

(a) Working Group on Mexican-American Agricultural Standards[8];
(b) Working Group on Canadian-Mexican Agricultural Standards[9]; and
(c) Working Group on Agricultural Subsidies[10].

---

2 NAFTA article 704.
3 NAFTA article 704. It should be noted that these policies will be affected by the Subsidies code contained in the Uruguay Round GATT.
4 NAFTA article 705(2).
5 NAFTA article 705(7)(b).
6 NAFTA article 705(4).
7 NAFTA article 706.
8 NAFTA annex 703.2, Section A, para. 25.
9 NAFTA annex 703.2, Section B, para. 13.
10 NAFTA article 705(6). The purpose of this working group is to work towards the elimination of export subsidies affecting agricultural trade between the Parties.

The NAFTA also creates an Advisory Committee on Private Commercial Disputes Regarding Agricultural Goods. This committee will report to the Committee on Agricultural Trade on the development of systems to provide prompt and effective dispute resolution[11].

2. AMERICAN-CANADIAN AGRICULTURAL TRADE

While the NAFTA does not contain a separate section dealing with American-Canadian agricultural trade, it does incorporate a number of agricultural trade provisions from the Canada-U.S. Free Trade Agreement[12]. These provisions relate to the following areas: agricultural export subsidies, temporary duties on fresh fruits and vegetables, quantitative restrictions on meat[13], import restrictions on goods containing less than 10 percent sugar by weight, and the rights of Parties under the GATT and definitions.

The dispute settlement provisions of the NAFTA will be used in the case of disagreements arising from these Canada-U.S. Free Trade Agreement provisions[14]. The NAFTA also preserves the GATT rights of the two Parties. This includes rights from the Protocol of Provisional Application and GATT waivers[15]. By preserving the GATT waivers, the United States has maintained all measures under s. 22 of the *Agricultural Adjustment Act*[16]. This section allows the President to impose fees, not exceeding 50 percent of the cost of the good, and quotas against imports that cause material injury to any program under the Act. The United States received a waiver for this program in 1955[17].

3. MEXICAN-AMERICAN AGRICULTURAL TRADE

The Mexican-American agricultural trade provisions apply to qualifying goods[18]. A qualifying good must meet the NAFTA rule of origin provisions strictly on the basis of its Mexican or American content[19].

---

11 NAFTA article 707.
12 NAFTA annex 702.1 incorporates articles 701, 702, 704, 705, 706, 707, 710 and 711 of the Canada-U.S. Free Trade Agreement. The NAFTA dispute settlement provisions will deal with agricultural disputes over these incorporated articles.
13 This will allow the United States to maintain those provisions of the *Meat Import Act of 1979*, under which it can impose quotas against Canadian meat imports.
14 NAFTA annex 702.1(3).
15 NAFTA annex 702.1(4).
16 *Agricultural Adjustment Act of 1933*, §22; 7 U.S.C.A. 624; *Agricultural Adjustment Act of 1956*, §204; 7 U.S.C.A. §1854.
17 GATT, BISD, 3 Supp. 32 (1955).
18 NAFTA annex 703.2, Section A, para. 2.
19 NAFTA annex 703.2, Section A, para. 26.

Agricultural goods which qualify for NAFTA inclusion will be able to take advantage of its benefits.

An important development contained in the NAFTA is its conversion of quantitative restriction into tariff-equivalents, such as TRQs[20]. Tariff-rate quotas are designed to assist producers of import sensitive products. Tariffs will not be imposed on imports which fit within the quota amount. Imports above the quota amount will attract an "over-quota duty" which will be at a higher rate[21]. A special provision in this chapter allows Mexico and the U.S. to impose over-quota tariffs at a level higher than their agreed GATT rates[22].

Mexico has converted its import licensing regime for imports of certain American goods, such as corn, eggs, wheat, barley, potatoes, milk, grapes, poultry, tobacco and dried beans from quotas to TRQ's[23]. In exchange, the United States has converted its import quotas under s. 22 of the *Agricultural Adjustment Act*[24] for dairy products, cotton, sugar-containing products and peanuts to TRQ's[25]. The U.S. has also agreed to waive fees to qualifying goods under s. 22[26].

Mexico and the United States eliminated tariffs on a large number of agricultural products. This will result in approximately one-half of U.S.-Mexico bilateral agricultural trade being duty-free. Mexican tariffs will immediately be eliminated on a number of agricultural products including:

- cattle;
- beef;
- hides and skins;
- fruits, vegetables, nuts;
- nursery products; and
- soybeans shipped between January and September.

All tariff barriers between Mexico and the United States will be eliminated no later than 10 years after the Agreement takes effect, with the exception of duties on certain highly-sensitive products. For Mexico, these sensitive products include corn and dry beans; for the United States, orange

---

20 This process is known as tariffication.

21 NAFTA annex 703.2, Section A, para. 4.

22 NAFTA annex 703.2, Section A, para. 4.

23 The U.S. administration suggests that between 1989 and 1991, 25 percent of the value of U.S. agricultural exports to Mexico were subject to these licenses. *Statement as to How the NAFTA Serves the Interest of United States Commerce*, appended to the *Statement of Administrative Action* at 12.

24 This is commonly known as a "section 22 action".

25 NAFTA annex 703.2, Section A, para. 8. Canada is still subject to these section 22 actions.

26 NAFTA annex 703.2, Section A, para. 2.

juice and sugar are considered sensitive. Tariff phase-outs on these few remaining products will be completed after 15 years.

Sugar proved to be a very sensitive issue for the American producers. Mexico and the United States will gradually liberalize their bilateral trade in sugar. The United States will allow an initial duty-free quota of 25,000 metric tonnes which will rise to 150,000 metric tonnes by 2001[27]. This quota is conditional on Mexico becoming a net exporter of sugar. Both countries will apply TRQ's of equivalent effect on third-country sugar by the sixth year of the Agreement[28]. For the first six years, the over-quota tariff for sugar will be reduced by 15 percent. All restrictions on trade in sugar between the two countries will be eliminated by the end of the 15-year transition period[29].

When either Mexico or the United States adopts measures regarding the classification, grading or marketing of a domestic agricultural product, the NAFTA requires that the Party will provide no less favourable treatment to like products imported from the other country for processing[30].

4. MEXICAN-CANADIAN AGRICULTURAL TRADE

The extent of the Mexican-Canadian deal is much smaller than the Mexican-American one due to the lower value of agricultural trade between these two countries. Average bilateral agricultural trade flows between 1989 and 1991 was $112 million from Canada to Mexico, and $150 million from Mexico to Canada. In addition, almost 85 percent of pre-NAFTA Mexican agricultural exports from Mexico to Canada were tariff-free[31].

Through the NAFTA, Canada and Mexico have agreed to eliminate all tariff and non-tariff barriers on their agricultural trade, with the exception of dairy, poultry, egg and sugar products[32]. Canada will immediately exempt Mexico from import restrictions covering wheat, barley and their byproducts, beef, veal, and margarine. Mexican tariffs will immediately be eliminated on the following:

- cattle;
- beef;
- rye;
- buckwheat;

27 NAFTA annex 703.2, Section A, para. 15.
28 NAFTA annex 703.2, Mexico-U.S., para. 15.
29 Other than sugar exported under the U.S. Sugar Re-Export Programs which will remain subject to MFN tariff rates.
30 NAFTA annex 703.2, Section A, para. 23.
31 *Inside U.S. Trade*, Aug. 21, 1992 at 20.
32 NAFTA annex 703.2, Section B, para. 7.

- frozen blueberries; and
- raspberries.

Canada and Mexico will eliminate immediately, or phase out within five years, tariffs on selected fruit and vegetable products, while tariffs on remaining fruit and vegetable products will be phased out over 10 years. Other than in the dairy, poultry and egg sectors, Mexico will replace its import licenses with tariffs, for example on wheat, or TRQ's, for example respecting corn and barley. These tariffs will generally be phased out over a 10-year period.

B. SANITARY AND PHYTOSANITARY MEASURES

The NAFTA Agriculture chapter includes an entire sub-chapter dedicated to sanitary and phytosanitary (SPS) measures that could affect trade between the Parties[33]. The term "sanitary and phytosanitary measures" refers to measures taken by governments for the protection of humans, animals or plants from pests, diseases, or contaminants. The NAFTA provisions do not in themselves impose any specific standards upon Parties. Instead, they set out a general approach to ensure that SPS measures are taken for scientific reasons rather than trade-protection ones.

The SPS provisions are in one of two NAFTA chapters which deal with standards-related measures[34]. Each chapter establishes an objective standard by which government measures are assessed. In the Technical Barriers chapter, the test is based on non-discrimination. In the SPS sub-chapter, discrimination between national and domestic goods is not the standard; rather, it is scientific fact and risk assessment[35]. This standard reflects the right of NAFTA Parties to take SPS measures to protect human, animal or plant life or health while also attempting to prevent the use of these measures as disguised barriers to trade.

1. BASIC RIGHTS AND OBLIGATIONS

The NAFTA confirms the right of each Party to set its SPS measures at levels that it considers appropriate[36]. Appropriate is defined by the Agreement to be[37]:

> the level of protection of human, animal or plant life or health in the territory of a Party that the Party considers appropriate.

---

33 NAFTA article 709.
34 Chapter 7-B and chapter 9.
35 *Statement of Administrative Action* at 88 makes this point.
36 NAFTA article 712(1).
37 NAFTA article 712(2).

The NAFTA commits its Parties to base SPS measures policy solely on scientific principles[38]. If the scientific basis underpinning a measure is no longer valid, then Parties are committed to changing the measure[39]. The *Statement of Administrative Action* has examined the question of what constitutes a scientific basis. It states[40]:

> The question is also *not* whether the measure was based on the "best" science or the "preponderance" of science or whether there was conflicting science. The question is only whether the government maintaining the measure has *a scientific* basis for it. This is because section B is based on a recognition that there is seldom, if ever, scientific certainty and consequently any scientific determination may require a judgment among differing scientific opinions. The NAFTA preserves the ability of *governments* to continue to make those judgments.

Parties may arrive at their appropriate level of SPS protection through measures that are applied only to the extent necessary to provide a country's chosen level of protection[41] and which do not result in unfair discrimination or disguised restrictions on trade[42].

(a) USE OF INTERNATIONAL STANDARDS

The NAFTA encourages its Parties to harmonize their measures based on relevant international standards[43]. A sanitary and phytosanitary measure that conforms to an international standard will be presumed to be consistent with the NAFTA SPS obligations[44]. Since the measure is exempt from challenge by a NAFTA Party, this presumption creates a strong incentive on a Party to accept harmonization based on international standards.

The sub-chapter places a focus on the scientific basis for a Party's SPS measures. This suggests that the only legitimate basis for applying NAFTA-consistent SPS measures is scientific. However, it permits each Party to adopt more stringent, scientifically-based measures when necessary to achieve its chosen level of protection[45]. The NAFTA Parties are committed to participate in, and review the international SPS standards from such international standardizing organizations as[46]:

---

38 NAFTA article 712(3)(a).
39 NAFTA article 712(3)(b).
40 *Statement of Administrative Action* at 93.
41 NAFTA article 712(5).
42 NAFTA article 712(6).
43 NAFTA article 713(2).
44 NAFTA article 713(2).
45 NAFTA article 713(3).
46 NAFTA article 713(5). This list provides examples of international or North American standardizing organizations that could also provide appropriate standards.

- the Codex Alimentarius Commission;
- the International Office of Epizootics;
- the Tripartite Animal Health Commission;
- the International Plant Protection Convention; and
- the North American Plant Protection Organization.

A difficulty raised by some environmentalists is that the standards set by international standardizing bodies afford lower levels of protection, in some cases, than existing domestic standards. Measures which exceed these international standards are subject to being justified on the basis of scientific criteria.

(b) RELATION TO OTHER NAFTA CHAPTERS

The provisions in the Market Access for Goods chapter regarding national treatment and import and export restrictions[47] do not apply to SPS measures. This allows governments to impose SPS measures on specific goods from a specific territory. The NAFTA also states that the NAFTA exception regarding the protection of human, animal and plant life or health[48] does not apply to this sub-chapter[49].

(c) HARMONIZATION AND EQUIVALENCE

Different governments may adopt different standards as they attempt to obtain the same level of SPS protection. NAFTA Parties have agreed to work toward equivalence in SPS measures without reducing any Party's level of protection of human, animal or plant life or health. The NAFTA permits the sanitary and phytosanitary measures of other Parties to be accepted as equivalent if they meet domestic levels of protection[50]. It also encourages the Parties to pursue equivalence in SPS standards to the greatest extent practicable[51].

The NAFTA gives an advantage to a Party that wishes to justify its choice of SPS measure before a NAFTA dispute panel. The NAFTA requires that any Party that challenges the NAFTA-consistency of a sanitary or phytosanitary measure has the burden of establishing the inconsistency[52]. This is a change of onus from that contained in the GATT or the Canada-U.S. Free Trade Agreement.

---

47 That is NAFTA articles 301 and 309.
48 NAFTA article 2101 incorporates GATT Article XX(B).
49 NAFTA article 710.
50 NAFTA article 714.
51 NAFTA article 713(5).
52 NAFTA article 723(6).

(d) RISK ASSESSMENT

The NAFTA does not set out a precise method for holding risk assessments of sanitary and phytosanitary measures. Risk assessment is defined by the agreement as being an evaluation of[53]:

(a) the potential introduction or spread of a pest or disease; or

(b) the potential for adverse effects on human or animal or plant life or [or] health arising from the presence of an additive, contaminant, toxin or disease-causing organism in a food, beverage or feedstuff.

When conducting a risk assessment, NAFTA Parties are committed to take into account the following[54]:

- relevant risk assessment techniques developed by North American standardizing organizations;
- relevant scientific evidence;
- relevant processes and production techniques;
- the prevalence of diseases or pests;
- relevant ecological and other environmental conditions; and
- relevant treatments such as quarantines.

While Parties may adopt whatever level of protection that they deem appropriate, the NAFTA does impose certain minimum requirements on measures. Parties are obliged to[55]:

- take into account the objective of minimizing negative trade effects; and
- avoid arbitrary or unjustifiable distinctions in levels of protection if these distinctions result in arbitrary or unjustifiable discrimination against goods from another NAFTA Party.

If a Party conducting a risk assessment is unable to complete an assessment due to insufficient information, it may adopt a provisional SPS measure. In such case, the Party must complete its study within a reasonable period of time after introduction[56].

(e) ADAPTATION TO REGIONAL CONDITIONS

Pests and diseases do not know of national borders when they strike. In order to deal with problems which are endemic to certain regions, the NAFTA allows governments to adapt their SPS measures to various re-

---

53 NAFTA article 724.
54 NAFTA article 715(1).
55 NAFTA article 715(3).
56 NAFTA article 715(4).

gional conditions[57]. When determining whether an area is pest-free, governments can take account of factors such as geography, ecosystems and the effectiveness of sanitary and phytosanitary controls[58]. The NAFTA prohibits discrimination against agricultural goods produced in a pest-free or disease-free area or area of low pest or disease prevalence[59].

(f) PROCEDURAL TRANSPARENCY

One of the general objectives of the NAFTA is to increase transparency and procedural due process in its Parties. The NAFTA requires that its federal-level governments provide public notice at least 60 days in advance, prior to the adoption or modification of any SPS measures[60]. In order to allow interested parties to have knowledge of what is required, the notice must identify the goods to be covered, and the objectives of and reasons for the measure.

Each NAFTA Party is required to name an "inquiry point" who will provide relevant information regarding SPS measures and risk assessment procedures[61]. National governments are required to take appropriate measures to ensure that state or provincial governments abide by the notification and publication guidelines including giving early notice of measures and allowing for comments from other Parties and other interested persons[62].

(g) CONTROL, INSPECTION AND APPROVAL PROCEDURES

The NAFTA explicitly allows governments the right to maintain approval procedures for goods containing additives entering their domestic markets until these goods have been suitably tested[63]. Other provisions allow for NAFTA governments to maintain control and inspection procedures for goods[64].

---

57 NAFTA article 716(1).
58 NAFTA article 716(3).
59 NAFTA article 716(5).
60 NAFTA article 718(1).
61 NAFTA article 719.
62 NAFTA article 718(2).
63 NAFTA article 717(4).
64 NAFTA article 717(1).

2. COMMITTEE ON SANITARY AND PHYTOSANITARY MEASURES

The NAFTA creates a Committee on Sanitary and Phytosanitary Measures comprised of government representatives who have responsibility for SPS measures. The Committee may facilitate consultations between the Parties over disputes based on SPS measures[65]. These consultations will constitute Party-to-Party consultations required by the NAFTA dispute settlement process[66].

---

65 NAFTA article 723(2).
66 NAFTA articles 723(5) and 2006.

8

Emergency Action

It is common for trade agreements to provide an opt-out clause which allows for the temporary suspension of benefits in circumstances where injury is occurring to the domestic economy as a result of a provision in the agreement, such as tariff modifications. This opt-out is known as either a safeguard or escape-clause action. Safeguard actions provide a means of allowing for economic adjustment when injury is being experienced by domestic industries. As such, they are an important tool of domestic industrial policy[1]. Safeguard actions are permitted by the GATT[2], the Canada-U.S. Free Trade Agreement[3] and the NAFTA[4]. In addition to these agreements, the NAFTA Parties agreed to a further trilateral understanding on import surges on September 14, 1993.

The NAFTA envisions two different safeguard situations: the first is caused by the impact of tariff phase-outs contained within the NAFTA. This is termed a bilateral safeguard. The second relates to imports from all sources and is termed a global safeguard.

1. BILATERAL SAFEGUARDS

Bilateral safeguards may be taken where a surge in imports is the substantial cause of serious injury to domestic producers[5]. The surge in imports must be the direct cause of the injury. This bilateral action is available for a transition period until 2004 for almost all goods covered by the NAFTA[6]. For Canadian and American disputes, the terms of article 1101 of the Canada-U.S. Free Trade Agreement apply, except for textile and apparel goods[7]. It requires an actual finding of injury before a safeguard

---

1 A good discussion of the policy reasons for, and usage of safeguard actions is provided by John Jackson in his book, *The World Trading System: Law and Policy of International Economic Relations.* (Cambridge, Mass: MIT Press, 1991) at 149-187.
2 GATT Article XIX.
3 Canada-U.S. Free Trade Agreement Chapter 11.
4 NAFTA chapter 8.
5 NAFTA article 801.
6 NAFTA article 804 defines the time period as being 10 years, except for goods in staging category C+ of the schedule of annex 302.2.
7 NAFTA annex 801.1(1).

action can take place. For Mexico, a safeguard action may commence if there is harm or a threat of serious harm.

In the safeguard action, the NAFTA Party may temporarily "snapback" the tariff reduction contained in the NAFTA or may increase the rate of tariff applied but never beyond the Most-Favoured-Nation rate. A bilateral safeguard action may only be taken for three years with an ability to add an additional year for serious situations.

2. GLOBAL SAFEGUARDS

The NAFTA establishes a second provision which allows a NAFTA Party to take a safeguard action against products from all countries. Global safeguard actions must be consistent with Article XIX of the GATT, which allows for tariff and quota-based safeguards. In the past, Canadian and Mexican producers have suffered harm from being "side-swiped" by American global safeguard actions. To accommodate the concerns of these trading partners, the NAFTA requires that Parties are to be exempted from global safeguards unless a NAFTA Party either:

(a) accounts for a substantial share of the imports; or

(b) imports from the exporting Party contribute importantly to the serious injury or the threat of serious injury.

A NAFTA Party will not "normally" account[8] for a substantial share of imports if it is not one of the top five suppliers of that good.

Because of the size and purchasing power of its market, safeguard actions taken by the United States can have a significant impact on its trading partners. One of the motivations for Mexico and Canada to enter into comprehensive trading relationships with the United States was to avoid being "sideswiped" during global safeguard actions. While the NAFTA purports to give protection, the use of the term "normally" raises some questions as to the extent of this protection NAFTA Parties may actually have. The American *Statement of Administrative Action* suggests how the administration views this term. It states[9]:

> As the use of the modifier "normally" makes clear, there likely will be instances when it is appropriate for the ITC to find that a NAFTA country accounts for a substantial share of total imports even though the country is not one of the top five suppliers. For example, when there is little difference between the share of the fifth-place supplier and those that fall below fifth place. . .

---

8 NAFTA article 802(2)(a).
9 *Statement of Administrative Action* at 116.

If a NAFTA Party is not included in an initial safeguard action, that Party may be added later if a surge in imports from that country undermines the effectiveness of the action.

3. PROCEDURAL REQUIREMENTS

NAFTA Parties have agreed to abide by procedural obligations which are based on those in GATT Article XIX. These provide transparency and equity in safeguard investigations carried out by the investigating authority[10]. Basic procedural requirements regarding the contents of petitions, the holding of public hearings and the making of decisions are included in the chapter[11].

The NAFTA prohibits the establishment of a dispute settlement panel based on a proposed safeguard action[12]. Presumably, a panel may be convened to deal with an actual safeguard situation.

In September 1993, the NAFTA Parties agreed to a trilateral *Understanding Concerning Emergency Action*. The Understanding provides for a consultative process regarding safeguard actions and for the creation of a Working Group on Emergency Actions. The Working Group will be able to consider the recourse of any Party to a safeguard action[13]. If the Parties agree, these consultations can constitute the consultations required by NAFTA articles 801 and 802[14].

---

10 In the United States, the International Trade Commission (ITC) is the relevant authority. In Canada, it is the Canadian International Trade Commission and in Mexico, the Ministry of Trade and Industrial Development.

11 NAFTA annex 803.3.

12 NAFTA article 804.

13 *Understanding between the Parties to the North American Free Trade Agreement Concerning Chapter Eight-Emergency Action*, article 3.

14 *Understanding between the Parties to the North American Free Trade Agreement Concerning Chapter Eight-Emergency Action*, article 3(D).

9
Technical Standards

Technical standards have been used as discriminatory barriers to international trade for centuries. They have served as useful non-tariff barriers that give an ostensibly objective reason for the arbitrary denial of market access. Yet technical standards also are an essential element of the national sovereignty that allows governments to take measures to protect the moral, environmental and fiscal health of their citizenry. With the advent of freer trade, technical barriers have become one of the principal forms of trade discrimination available to governments. Often these barriers have been used in an unjustified manner. For example, Professor John Jackson relates the example of a requirement that French inspectors must inspect the production site of all pharmaceuticals sold in France. This measure turns into a barrier when it is coupled with the fact that French inspectors do not travel abroad[1].

In light of such longstanding barriers, the NAFTA negotiators found themselves grappling with two competing values. They were forced to weigh the protection of national sovereignty against the objective of free trade. It is not surprising to find that the resulting chapter displays elements of both.

1. SCOPE

The NAFTA defines standards-related measures to consist of three types of measures: standards, technical regulations and conformity assessments[2]. The term "standards" refers to voluntary product standards while "technical regulations" refers to mandatory standards imposed by governments. "Conformity assessments" refer to procedures which determine whether a product meets the standard or technical regulation[3].

The NAFTA Technical Standards chapter applies to all standards-related matters that, directly or indirectly, affect trade in goods or services,

---

1 *The World Trading System* at 197, n. 27. Professor Jackson provides other examples of barriers which operate in a discriminatory fashion.
2 NAFTA article 915.
3 *Statement of Administrative Action* at 121.

other than agricultural and procurement standards which are dealt with in their own NAFTA chapters[4]. The NAFTA commitments apply directly to the national governments of each Party. In addition, this chapter has its own unique extent of obligations commitment. National governments are obliged to take all appropriate measures to ensure observance of the technical standards obligations[5] by state and provincial governments and nongovernment standardizing bodies[6]. The NAFTA Parties agreed to an apparently lesser commitment on account of the many considerations which could lead their subnational governments to arrive at different levels of technical standards[7].

2. COMMITMENTS

The NAFTA builds upon the earlier commitments established by the GATT and the Canada-U.S. Free Trade Agreement. The GATT national treatment obligation does not speak to issues regarding the equivalency of standards. During the Tokyo Round, the GATT Parties agreed upon a code on Technical Barriers to Trade[8]. It provided that Parties should not take measures which had the effect of arbitrary or unjustified discrimination between imported and domestic goods[9]. This code established procedures for the resolution of disputes based on technical barriers to trade.

The Canada-U.S. Free Trade Agreement expanded upon the commitments in the GATT Technical Barriers Code. The Canadian-American Agreement established additional procedural guarantees based on the principles of increasing compatibility and mutual recognition of standards[10].

The NAFTA attempts to ensure that any difference in technical standards is based on legitimate policy differences rather than being an attempt to discriminate against foreign goods. At the same time, each Party retains the right to adopt, apply and enforce standards-related measures that result in a higher level of protection than would be achieved by measures based on international standards. The NAFTA establishes four basic standards-related obligations:

---

4 NAFTA article 901.
5 That is, articles 904 to 908.
6 The NAFTA extent of obligation provisions are discussed more fully in chapter 2 of this book.
7 The *Statement of Administrative Action* alludes to the choice of this lower standard. At 124, it states "Article 902(2) is intended to reflect a lesser level of obligation than that found in GATT Article XXIV:12, as it has recently been interpreted".
8 GATT, BISD, 26 Supp. 8 (1980).
9 GATT Technical Barriers Code, article 2.1.
10 Canada-U.S. Free Trade Agreement chapter 6.

(a) RIGHT TO TAKE STANDARDS-RELATED MEASURES

NAFTA Parties may adopt, apply and enforce standards-related measures, including measures relating to "safety, the protection of human, animal or plant life or health, the environment or consumers"[11]. Parties are able to adopt, maintain, or apply standards-related measures which prohibit the import of a good or service from another Party that does not comply with domestic standards.

(b) RIGHT TO ESTABLISH A LEVEL OF PROTECTION

Each Party may choose the appropriate level of protection it wishes to achieve and to conduct assessments of risk to ensure that those levels are achieved[12]. In setting this level, Parties are to avoid unjustifiable discrimination against the goods of another Party[13].

(c) NON-DISCRIMINATION

Each Party must extend national treatment and Most-Favoured Nation treatment in its standards-related measures. Goods and services from other NAFTA Parties must be treated as favourably as those which are domestic, or which come from non-NAFTA Party countries[14].

(d) UNNECESSARY OBSTACLES

NAFTA Parties may not create or use standards-related measures as an unnecessary obstacle to trade. Parties are required to show that the demonstrable purpose of their standards-related measure is to achieve a legitimate objective, and that the measure does not exclude goods of other Parties that meet the objective[15]. The NAFTA defines a legitimate objective as including objectives such as safety; the protection of human, animal or plant life or health; and sustainable development[16]. Because of its permissive wording, a legitimate objective is not limited to these items. The NAFTA specifies that an international standard, used by a Party as a technical

---

11 NAFTA article 904(1). This language is identical to much of the language contained in the GATT Technical Barriers Code, article 2.1.
12 NAFTA article 904(2).
13 NAFTA article 907(2).
14 NAFTA article 904(3).
15 NAFTA article 904(4).
16 NAFTA article 915.

standard, is presumed to be consistent with the chapter's obligations that technical barriers not constitute an unnecessary obstacle to trade[17]. The NAFTA attempts to weigh the competing values of trade liberalization and the maintenance of high standards. For example, article 906(1) states:

> Recognizing the crucial role of standards-related measures in achieving legitimate objectives, the Parties shall, in accordance with this Chapter, work jointly to enhance the level of safety and of protection of human, animal and plant life and health, the environment and consumers.

The Agreement is always careful to balance its provisions on trade liberalization with offsetting concessions on the ability of governments to maintain standards. This results in provisions which may not provide for a great deal of progress on either front. For example, Parties are committed to work jointly to enhance the level of safety, health, environmental and consumer protection. The NAFTA provides that, without reducing the level of safety or protection and taking into account international standards, Parties will make their standards-related measures compatible to the greatest extent practicable[18]. This type of a provision attempts to deal with both sides of the balance at the same time.

The NAFTA attempts to have standards established on a non-discriminatory basis. Wherever possible, standards are to be based on international practice with the standards set by standardizing bodies. This commitment is softened by including a proviso that it need not be met where such standards would be an ineffective or inappropriate means to fulfil that government's legitimate objective[19].

It should be noted that the NAFTA provides that a Party that challenges the consistency of another Party's standards-related measure has the burden of proving the inconsistency of that measure with the NAFTA[20]. This provides a significant procedural advantage to standard-setters over challengers.

(e) CONFORMITY ASSESSMENT

The NAFTA provides for conformity assessments which will determine whether standards-related measures have been met. The NAFTA sets out a list of rules governing these procedures to ensure that they do not create unnecessary obstacles to trade. Parties have agreed, wherever possible, to accept the results of a conformity assessment conducted by another

---

17 NAFTA article 905(2).
18 NAFTA article 906(2).
19 NAFTA article 905(1).
20 NAFTA article 914(4).

Party as if it had taken place in their own[21]. Parties will consult in advance to agree on the reliability of each other's procedures for these tests[22]. The NAFTA allows its Parties the right to conduct risk assessments in order to set standards[23]. If a Party relies on the risk assessment, it "should avoid arbitrary or unjustifiable discrimination between similar goods or services"[24].

(f) TRANSPARENCY ISSUES

Like in other areas of the Agreement, the NAFTA provides for due process and transparency rights for its Parties. The Agreement imposes strict minimum requirements on the actions of governments related to the making of new standards-related measures. The NAFTA requires public notice at least 60 days prior to the adoption of modification of standards-related measures that may affect trade in the NAFTA zone[25]. Such notice must identify the good or service to be affected and the objectives of, and the reasons for the measure. Parties and affected individuals may comment on these measures. A NAFTA Party may not charge a greater price to a foreigner for documents relating to its NAFTA standards obligations than it would charge to its own nationals[26]. In addition, Parties are required to identify "inquiry points" to answer all reasonable inquiries and provide relevant documents[27]. They are required to provide technical advice, information and assistance on mutually-agreed terms and conditions at the request of another Party[28]. Parties will also encourage their domestic standardizing bodies to cooperate with standardizing bodies in other Parties[29].

3. COMMITTEE ON STANDARDS-RELATED MEASURES

The NAFTA creates a Committee on Standards-Related Measures which is comprised of Party representatives. The committee will monitor the implementation and administration of this chapter and review the work of standards-related working groups. The committee may facilitate consultations between NAFTA Parties on disputes raised regarding standards-

---

21 NAFTA article 906(6).
22 NAFTA article 906(7).
23 NAFTA article 907(1).
24 NAFTA article 907(2).
25 This time period is reduced to 30 days for measures relating to perishable goods.
26 NAFTA article 910(4).
27 NAFTA article 910.
28 NAFTA article 911(1).
29 NAFTA article 911(2).

related measures. These consultations will constitute the Party-to-Party consultations required by the NAFTA dispute resolution process[30]. The Committee on Standards-Related Measures is required to meet at least once a year and report annually to the Free Trade Commission[31].

The NAFTA has established four subcommittees of the Committee on Standards-Related Measures[32]. They are:

(1) Land Transportation Standards Subcommittee;

(2) Telecommunications Standards Subcommittee;

(3) Automotive Standards Council Subcommittee; and

(4) Subcommittee on Labelling of Textile and Apparel Goods.

The committee may create other subcommittees as necessary. All of these subcommittees and working groups may invite the participation of scientists and representatives of interested non-governmental organizations from the three countries[33].

---

30 NAFTA articles 913(2)(c) and 2006.

31 NAFTA article 913(3).

32 NAFTA article 913(5).

33 NAFTA article 913(4).

10

Government Procurement

Government procurement of goods and services in the three NAFTA countries amounts to approximately $800 million dollars annually[1]. With such a large potential market to access, it is not surprising that the NAFTA contains an entire chapter on this topic. Creating access to government procurement has always been a difficult matter for trade agreements. For example, within the original GATT text, there is no provision on government procurement[2]. Only in its third decade of operation could the GATT Parties even reach agreement on the wording of an optional GATT Code to cover government procurement[3].

The NAFTA Procurement chapter builds upon the precedent of the GATT Code and the Canada-U.S. Free Trade Agreement's chapter 13 on procurement. However, neither of these codes applied to Mexico. The NAFTA marks the first time that the government of Mexico has ever participated in an agreement to eliminate restrictions against foreigners in its government procurement.

1. EARLIER AGREEMENTS

The GATT Procurement Code listed government entities which are obligated to abide by its obligations for purchases in excess of US $171,000[4]. The code also contained specific rules to provide for transparency and procedural fairness in tendering and in the review of the bidding process.

The Canada-U.S. Free Trade Agreement also contained regulations regarding threshold amounts, tendering obligations and bid review for government procurement. This bilateral agreement reduced the threshold amount for covered entities to US $25,000.

---

1 *NAFTA: What's It All About?* (Ottawa: Government of Canada, Department of External Affairs and International Trade, 1993) at 58.

2 Article III:8(a) of the GATT exempted government procurement.

3 Agreement on Government Procurement, GATT, BISD, 26 Supp. 33 (1980).

4 Article 1(1)(b) of the GATT Procurement Code actually sets the threshold level at SDR 150,000 which is equivalent to approximately US $171,000. In 1986, this threshold was lowered to SDR 130,000. GATT, BISD, 33 Supp. 190 (1987).

The Canada-U.S. Free Trade Agreement covered only a small portion of the total procurement market in both countries. Only entities at the federal level were listed, so that the vast state, provincial and municipal procurement markets were avoided[5]. In addition, a number of key areas were carved out of the scope of the agreement, such as services.

2. THE NAFTA

The NAFTA covers procurement by specified federal departments and federally controlled state enterprises. Procurement is defined very broadly by the NAFTA to cover not only the sale of goods and services[6], but also leases and rentals[7]. Procurement does not extend to government assistance such as subsidies or non-contractual agreements[8].

The NAFTA addresses itself to two types of government purchasers: governments themselves and government-owned enterprises. For those listed areas of the federal level of government, the NAFTA applies to procurements of over US $50,000 for goods and services[9]. The NAFTA marks the first time that an international trading agreement has applied to construction services. It applies to government procurement of construction services in excess of US $6.5 million. For federal government enterprises, the NAFTA applies to procurements of over US $250,000 for goods and services and over US $8 million for construction services[10].

Because of the application of the Agreement to government enter- prises, Canadian and American businesses will now have access to procure- ments made by Mexican *parastatals*[11] like PEMEX, the state-run petroleum enterprise and the Comision Federal de Electricidad (CFE), the state-run electricity enterprise. The NAFTA creates access to 59 percent of the procurement of these parastatals immediately, with increasing access avail- able over time until the year 2002[12].

In the United States, a number of new entities were covered by the procurement provisions of the NAFTA. Mexican and Canadian enterprises must now be granted access to four new government departments and

---

5 NAFTA article 1001(1)(a) as modified by annex 1001.1a-3.
6 The NAFTA Procurement chapter only applies to services listed in the temporary schedule in NAFTA annex 1001.1b-2. Mexico is required to list its exceptions to the Procurement chapter in this annex by July 1, 1995.
7 NAFTA article 1001(5).
8 NAFTA article 1001(5)(a).
9 NAFTA article 1001(1)(c)(i).
10 NAFTA article 1001(1)(c)(ii).
11 Parastatals are Mexican government-owned and operated enterprises.
12 NAFTA annex 1001.2a.

several government enterprises under the procurement obligations of the GATT:

- Department of Energy;
- Department of Transportation;
- Army Corps of Engineers[13];
- Bureau of Reclamation;
- Tennessee Valley Authority;
- St. Lawrence Seaway Development Corp.; and
- Marketing Administrations of the Department of Energy[14].

In addition, the NAFTA requires the United States to waive application of its *Buy America Act* restrictions on all procurements covered by the NAFTA chapter. Small and minority business set asides were also exempted from the procurement rules[15].

The NAFTA continues all commitments contained in the Canada-U.S. Free Trade Agreement's Procurement chapter[16]. The NAFTA procurement obligations do not apply to procurements for arms, ammunition, weapons and other national security procurements[17].

The NAFTA's general exceptions clause in article 2101 does not apply to the Procurement chapter. Thus, this chapter sets out its own exceptions provisions. The Agreement states that nothing will prevent a Party from taking measures:

(a) necessary to protect public morals, order or safety;

(b) necessary to protect human, animal or plant life or health;

(c) necessary to protect intellectual property; or

(d) relating to goods or services of handicapped persons, of philanthropic institutions or of prison labour.

Such measures may only be taken if they do not constitute a means of arbitrary or unjustifiable discrimination where the same conditions prevail, or a disguised restriction on trade[18].

(a) GENERAL OBLIGATIONS

The NAFTA Procurement chapter commits the covered entities of Parties to provide the goods and services of another Party treatment no less

---

13 The Canadian *Statement of Government Action* states that the addition of the Army Corps of Engineers adds a new procurement market of nearly US $9 billion alone (at 141).

14 This is pointed out in the *Statement of Administrative Action* at 138.

15 NAFTA annex 1001.2b, Schedule of the United States, para. 1.

16 Canada-U.S. Free Trade Agreement chapter 13.

17 NAFTA article 1018.

18 NAFTA article 1018(2).

favourably than that given to domestic goods, services and suppliers[19]. Local suppliers which have an ownership interest by an investor from a NAFTA Party may not be treated less favourably than entirely domestically-owned local suppliers[20].

The Agreement does allow that, after consultations between the Parties, a Party can deny the NAFTA Procurement chapter benefits to a service-provider that is owned or controlled by non-NAFTA Party Investors and that has no substantial business activity in the territory of any Party[21].

Covered entities are prohibited from considering or imposing offsets when they evaluate bids from NAFTA Party enterprises[22]. Contractual conditions that require local content, licensing of technology, investment, counter-trade or other similar requirements are prohibited. Technical specifications also may not be used in a manner which could impose an unnecessary obstacle to trade[23].

(i) Tendering and Bid Review

The NAFTA establishes procedures to create a transparent, non-discriminatory process for tendering and bid review. The NAFTA sets out procedures which require advance publication of invitations to participate in a proposed procurement[24]. In addition, it sets out requirements regarding the qualification of suppliers[25], the time limits for tendering[26], requirements on documentation[27] and on how contracts are to be awarded[28]. Tendering which does not comply with these rules may only occur in limited circumstances[29].

Suppliers may apply to have the bidding process reviewed by an independent body in each country[30]. These rules are identical to the bid challenge procedure contained in article 1305 of the Canada-U.S. Free Trade Agreement. A bid challenge may be brought against any aspect of the procurement process[31]. A supplier must have at least 10 days to bring a

---

19 NAFTA article 1003.
20 NAFTA article 1003(2).
21 NAFTA article 1005.
22 NAFTA article 1006.
23 NAFTA article 1007.
24 NAFTA article 1010.
25 NAFTA article 1009.
26 NAFTA article 1012.
27 NAFTA article 1013.
28 NAFTA article 1015.
29 NAFTA article 1016.
30 NAFTA article 1017.
31 NAFTA article 1017(1).

challenge from the date of knowing, or reasonably knowing, the basis of the challenge[32].

(ii) Further Negotiations

The Parties are obligated to endeavour to extend the coverage to state and provincial governments by 1998[33]. In addition, all subsequent changes to procurement thresholds which occur in the GATT Code will automatically be incorporated into the NAFTA commitment[34]. As well, negotiations on electronic transmission of procurement information will commence between the Parties in 1995.

(iii) Covered Entities

The NAFTA sets out those entities listed by the NAFTA Parties, which are subject to the Agreement's procurement obligations. These entities are set out in annex 1001.1a-1 as follows:

Schedule of Canada

1. Department of Agriculture
2. Department of Communications
3. Department of Consumer and Corporate Affairs
4. Department of Employment and Immigration
5. Immigration and Refugee Board
6. Canada Employment and Immigration Commission
7. Department of Energy, Mines and Resources
8. Atomic Energy Control Board
9. National Energy Board
10. Department of the Environment
11. Department of External Affairs
12. Canadian International Development Agency (on its own account)
13. Department of Finance
14. Office of the Superintendent of Financial Institutions
15. Canadian International Trade Tribunal
16. Municipal Development and Loan Board
17. Department of Fisheries and Oceans
18. Department of Forestry
19. Department of Indian Affairs and Northern Development
20. Department of Industry, Science and Technology

---

32 NAFTA article 1017(1)(f).
33 NAFTA article 1024.
34 NAFTA article 1024(4)(a).

21. Science Council of Canada
22. National Research Council of Canada
23. Natural Sciences and Engineering Research Council of Canada
24. Department of Justice
25. Canadian Human Rights Commission
26. Statute Revision Commission
27. Supreme Court of Canada
28. Department of Labour
29. Canada Labour Relations Board
30. Department of National Health and Welfare
31. Medical Research Council
32. Department of National Revenue
33. Department of Public Works
34. Department of Secretary of State of Canada
35. Social Sciences and Humanities Research Council
36. Office of the Co-ordinator, Status of Women
37. Public Service Commission
38. Department of the Solicitor General
39. Correctional Service of Canada
40. National Parole Board
41. Department of Supply and Services (on its own account)
42. Canadian General Standards Board
43. Department of Transport (Pursuant to Article 1018, the national secu-
    rity considerations applicable to the Department of National Defence
    are equally applicable to the Canadian Coast Guard.)
44. Treasury Board Secretariat and the Office of the Controller General
45. Department of Veterans Affairs
46. Veterans Land Administration
47. Department of Western Economic Diversification
48. Atlantic Canada Opportunities Agency
49. Auditor General of Canada
50. Federal Office of Regional Development (Quebec)
51. Canadian Centre for Management Development
52. Canadian Radio-Television and Telecommunications Commission
53. Canadian Sentencing Commission
54. Civil Aviation Tribunal
55. Commission of Inquiry into the Air Ontario Crash at Dryden, Ontario
56. Commission of Inquiry into the Use of Drugs and Banned Practices
    Intended to Increase Athletic Performance
57. Commissioner for Federal Judicial Affairs
58. Competition Tribunal Registry
59. Copyright Board
60. Emergency Preparedness Canada

61. Federal Court of Canada
62. Grain Transportation Agency
63. Hazardous Materials Information Review Commission
64. Information and Privacy Commissioners
65. Investment Canada
66. Multiculturalism and Citizenship
67. The National Archives of Canada
68. National Farm Products Marketing Council
69. The National Library
70. National Transportation Agency
71. Northern Pipeline Agency
72. Patented Medicine Prices Review Board
73. Petroleum Monitoring Agency
74. Privy Council Office
75. Canadian Intergovernmental Conference Secretariat
76. Commissioner of Official Languages
77. Economic Council of Canada
78. Public Service Staff Relations Office
79. Office of the Secretary to the Governor General
80. Office of the Chief Electoral Officer
81. Federal Provincial Relations Office
82. Procurement Review Board
83. Royal Commission on Electoral Reform and Party Financing
84. Royal Commission on National Passenger Transportation
85. Royal Commission on New Reproductive Technologies
86. Royal Commission on the Future of the Toronto Waterfront
87. Statistics Canada
88. Tax Court of Canada, Registry of the
89. Agricultural Stabilization Board
90. Canadian Aviation Safety Board
91. Canadian Centre for Occupational Health and Safety
92. Canadian Transportation Accident Investigation and Safety Board
93. Director of Soldier Settlement
94. Director, The Veterans' Land Act
95. Fisheries Prices Support Board
96. National Battlefields Commission
97. Royal Canadian Mounted Police
98. Royal Canadian Mounted Police External Review Committee
99. Royal Canadian Mounted Police Public Complaints Commission
100. Department of National Defence

Schedule of Mexico

1. Secretaría de Gobernación (Ministry of Government)
   - Centro Nacional de Estudios Municipales (National Center for Municipal Studies)
   - Comisión Calificadora de Publicaciones y Revistas Ilustradas (Illustated Periodicals and Publications Classification Commission)
   - Consejo Nacional de Población (National Population Council)
   - Archivo General de la Nación (General Archives of the Nation)
   - Instituto Nacional de Estudios Históricos de la Revolución Mexicana (National Institute of Historical Studies on the Mexican Revolution)
   - Patronato de Asistencia para la Reincorporación Social (Social Reintegration Assistance Foundation)
   - Centro Nacional de Prevención de Desastres (National Disaster Prevention Center
   - Consejo Nacional de Radio y Televisión (National Radio and Television Council)
   - Comisión Mexicana de Ayuda a Refugiados (Mexican Commission on Refugee Assistance)
2. Secretaría de Relaciones Exteriores (Ministry of Foreign Relations)
   - Sección Mexicana de la Comisión Intercional de Límites y Aguas México-EEUU (Mexican Section of the International Boundary and Water Commission, Mexico and the United States)
   - Sección Mexicana de la Comisión Internacional de Límites y Aguas México-Guatemala (Mexican Section of the International Boundary and Water Commission, Mexico and Guatemala)
3. Secretaría de Hacienda y Crédito Público (Ministry of Finance and Public Credit
   - Comisión Nacional Bancaria (National Banking Commission)
   - Comisión Nacional de Valores (National Securities Commission)
   - Comisión Nacional de Seguros y Fianzas (National Insurance and Bonds Commission)
   - Instituto Nacional de Estadística, Geografía e Informática (National Institute of Stastics, Geography, and Informatics)
4. Secretaría de Agricultura y Recursos Hidráulicos (Ministry of Agriculture and Water Resources)
   - Instituto Mexicano de Tecnología del Agua (Mexican Institute of Water Technology)
   - Instituto Nacional de Investigaciones Forestales y Agropecuarias (National Forestry and Agricultural Research Institute)
   - Apoyos a Servicios a la Comercialización Agropecuaria (Aserca) (Support Services for Agricultural Marketing)

5. Secretaría de Comunicaciones y Transportes (including the Instituto Mexicano de Comunicaciones and the Instituto Mexicano de Transporte) (Ministry of Communications and Transport, including the Mexican Institute of Communications and the Mexican Institute of Transportation)

6. Secretaría de Comercio y Fomento Industrial (Ministry of Commerce and Industrial Development)

7. Secretaría de Educación Pública (Ministry of Public Education)
   — Instituto Nacional de Antropología e Historia (National Institute of Anthropology and History)
   — Instituto Nacional de Bellas Artes y Literatura (National Institute of Fine Arts and Literature)
   — Radio Educación (Radio Education)
   — Centro de Ingeniería y Desarrollo Industrial (Engineering and Industrial Development Center)
   — Consejo Nacional para la Cultura y las Artes (National Council for Culture and the Arts)
   — Comisión Nacional del Deporte (National Sports Commission)

8. Secretaría de Salud (Ministry of Health)
   — Administración del Patrimonio de la Beneficencia Pública (Public Charity Fund Administration)
   — Centro Nacional de la Transfusión Sanguínea (National Blood Transfusion Center)
   — Gerencia General de Biológicos y Reactivos (Office of General Management for Biological and Reagents)
   — Centro para el Desarrollo de la Infraestructura en Salud (Center for Infrastructural Development in Health)
   — Instituto de la Comunicación Humana Dr. Andrés Bustamante Gurría (Dr. Andrés Bustamante Gurría Institute of Human Communication)
   — Instituto Nacional de Medicina de la Rehabilitación (National Rehabilitative Medicine Institute)
   — Instituto Nacional de Ortopedia (National Orthopedics Institute)
   — Consejo Nacional para la Prevención y Control del Síndrome de la Inmunodeficiencia Adquirida, Conasida (National Council for the Prevention and Control of the Acquired Immune Deficiency Syndrome)

9. Secretaría del Trabajo y Previsión Social (Ministry of Labor and Social Welfare)
   — Procuraduría Federal de la Defensa del Trabajo (Office of the Federal Attorney for Labor Defense)

10. Secretaría de la Reforma Agraria (Ministry of Agrarian Reform)
    — Instituto de Capacitación Agraria (Institute of Agricultural Training)
11. Secretaría de Pesca (Ministry of Fisheries)
    — Instituto Nacional de la Pesca (National Institute of Fisheries)
12. Procuraduría General de la República (Office of the Attorney General of the Republic)
13. Secretaría de Energía Minas e Industria Paraestatal (Ministry of Energy, Mines, and Parastatal Industry)
    — Comisión Nacional de Seguridad Nuclear y Salvaguardias (National Commission on Nuclear Safety and Safeguards)
    — Comisión Nacional para el Ahorro de Energía (National Commission for Energy Conservation)
14. Secretaría de Desarrollo Social (Ministry of Social Development)
15. Secretaría de Turismo (Ministry of Tourism)
16. Secretaría de la Contraloría General de La Federación (Ministry of the Comptroller General of the Federation)
17. Comisión Nacional de Zonas Aridas (National Commission on Arid Zones)
18. Comisión Nacional de Libros de Texto Gratuito (National Commission on Free Textbooks)
19. Comisión Nacional de Derechos Humanos (National Commission on Human Rights)
20. Consejo Nacional de Fomento Educativo (National Educational Development Council)
21. Secretaría de la Defensa Nacional (Ministry of National Defense)
22. Secretaría de Marina (Ministry of the Navy)

Notes:
1. **This Schedule covers the numbered entities and those listed thereunder.**
2. **Translation provided for purposes of reference only.**

Schedule of the United States

1. Department of Agriculture (Not including procurement of agricultural products made in furtherance of agricultural support programs or human feeding programs. Federal buy national requirements imposed as conditions of funding by the Rural Electrification Administration will not apply to products and services of Mexico and Canada.)
2. Department of Commerce
3. Department of Education
4. Department of Health and Human Services
5. Department of Housing and Urban Development

6. Department of the Interior, including the Bureau of Reclamation (For suppliers of goods and services of Canada, the obligations of this Chapter will apply to procurements by the Bureau of Reclamation of the Department of Interior only at such time as the obligations of this Chapter take effect for procurements by Canadian Provincial Hydro utilities.)
7. Department of Justice
8. Department of Labor
9. Department of State
10. United States Agency for International Development
11. Department of the Treasury
12. Department of Transportation (Pursuant to Article 1018, the national security considerations applicable to the Department of Defense are equally applicable to the Coast Guard, a military unit of the United States.)
13. Department of Energy (This Chapter does not apply, pursuant to Article 1018, to national security procurements made in support of safeguarding nuclear materials or technology and entered into under the authority of the Atomic Energy Act; and to oil purchases related to the Strategic Petroleum Reserve.)
14. General Services Administration (except Federal Supply Groups 51 and 52 and Federal Supply Class 7340)
15. National Aeronautics and Space Administration
16. The Department of Veterans Affairs
17. Environmental Protection Agency
18. United States Information Agency
19. National Science Foundation
20. Panama Canal Commission
21. Executive Office of the President
22. Farm Credit Administration
23. National Credit Union Administration
24. Merit Systems Protection Board
25. ACTION
26. United States Arms Control and Disarmament Agency
27. The Office of Thrift Supervision
28. The Federal Housing Finance Board
29. National Labor Relations Board
30. National Mediation Board
31. Railroad Retirement Board
32. American Battle Monuments Commission
33. Federal Communications Commission
34. Federal Trade Commission
35. Inter-State Commerce Commission

36. Securities and Exchange Commission
37. Office of Personnel Management
38. United States International Trade Commission
39. Export-Import Bank of the United States
40. Federal Mediation and Conciliation Service
41. Selective Service System
42. Smithsonian Institution
43. Federal Deposit Insurance Corporation
44. Consumer Product Safety Commission
45. Equal Employment Opportunity Commission
46. Federal Maritime Commission
47. National Transportation Safety Board
48. Nuclear Regulatory Commission
49. Overseas Private Investment Corporation
50. Administrative Conference of the United States
51. Board for International Broadcasting
52. Commission on Civil Rights
53. Commodity Futures Trading Commission
54. The Peace Corps
55. National Archives and Records Administration
56. Department of Defense, including the Army Corps of Engineers

11

Investment

The symbolism of placing the NAFTA Investment chapter at the centre of the agreement's text is not lost, for in terms of importance, these provisions constitute the very heart and soul of the NAFTA. The Investment chapter builds upon the precedent of the Canada-U.S. Free Trade Agreement[1], however the NAFTA greatly broadens the coverage and the governmental obligations of the earlier bilateral agreement. The NAFTA augments the approach of the Canada-U.S. Free Trade Agreement by imposing more extensive obligations and by creating a process for the binding settlement of investment disputes between NAFTA investors and other NAFTA governments.

Fundamentally, the NAFTA's Investment chapter does the following:

- it establishes common rules for the treatment of investment from investors of other NAFTA countries;
- it liberalizes existing investment restrictions; and
- it provides a mechanism to resolve investment disputes between investors and other NAFTA governments.

1. SCOPE OF THE INVESTMENT CHAPTER

The reach of the NAFTA Investment chapter is all encompassing. NAFTA article 1101 establishes that the Investment chapter applies to those measures relating to:

(a) investors of another Party; or
(b) the investments of investors of another Party in the territory of the host Party[2].

The structure of article 1101 must be considered in the context of the chapter's defined terms. The Investment chapter applies to a wide range of direct and indirect investments and to investments existing when the NAFTA went into force on January 1, 1994 and after. In the event of any

---

1 The Canada-U.S. Free Trade Agreement chapter 16.
2 NAFTA Interpretive note 38 specifies that investments existing on the date of entry into force of the Agreement as well as investments made or acquired after that date are covered by the investment obligations.

inconsistency between a provision of the Investment chapter and another chapter, the other provision will prevail to the extent of the inconsistency[3].

(a) THE DEFINITION OF INVESTMENT

It is impossible to comprehend the magnitude of the scope of NAFTA's investment obligations without reviewing the definition of its key terms. The term "investment" is broadly defined[4] to include virtually all types of ownership interests, either direct or indirect[5], actual or contingent. Under the NAFTA, investment could be defined as the following:

- a business[6];

- a share of a business;

- a debt security (like a convertible debenture) in a business which is an affiliate of the investor or where the security matures in more than three years[7];

- a loan to a business that is an affiliate of the investor or where the security matures in more than three years;

- any business interest that entitles an owner to share in the income or profits;

- any business interest that entitles an owner to share in the assets other than a debt security or a loan by a state enterprise;

- real estate or other property (tangible and intangible) acquired "in the expectation or used for the purpose of economic benefit or other business purposes";

- interests where there is a commitment of capital such as construction contracts, turnkey projects or concessions; and

---

3 NAFTA article 1112.
4 NAFTA article 1138.
5 This broad definition has followed the trend of recent international arbitral decisions such as those taken during the U.S.-Iran Claims Tribunal. A similar position has been taken in a number of bilateral investment treaties.
6 The actual NAFTA provision uses the term "enterprise" instead of the term "business". The term "enterprise" is a defined term in the NAFTA. Article 201 defines it to mean "any entity constituted or organized under applicable law, whether or not for profit, and whether privately-owned or governmentally-owned, including any corporation, trust, partnership, sole proprietorship, joint venture or other association."
7 Debt securities issued by state enterprises are not eligible to be treated as a NAFTA investment.

• interests where there is a commitment of capital and where remuneration depends substantially on production, revenues or profits.

In fact, the term "investment" is so broad, that the NAFTA includes a provision to determine what it does not mean. Investment does not include claims to money including claims arising from commercial contracts for the sale of goods or services between NAFTA Parties or the extension of credit[8] for trade financing. These "non-investment" claims may not involve the types of interests which are specifically considered as being investments[9].

In addition to defining the term investment, the NAFTA Investment chapter contains other key definitions. It defines an investor of a NAFTA Party to be either a Party itself, one of its state enterprises or a national of the Party. To have status as a NAFTA investor, the national need not actually have an investment, but could also receive investor status by seeking to be an investor[10]. The NAFTA defines an investment of an investor to mean any investment which is owned or directly or indirectly controlled by a NAFTA investor.

The Investment chapter contains certain exceptions. It does not apply to issues which are covered by the Financial Services chapter, however that chapter incorporates a number of the investment obligations[11]. Also, sectors listed by Parties in NAFTA annex III are exempt from the chapter. Mexico has also exempted investments in petroleum, energy, nuclear power, and communications from the NAFTA's investment obligations[12].

Parties also have a right to make "bound" reservations for non-conforming subnational measures which were in existence on January 1, 1994. These reservations may only be taken by January 1, 1996. Each NAFTA Party has also made general "unbound reservations" in NAFTA annex II which allows it to continue to make policies in these specific areas unimpeded by NAFTA obligations[13].

---

8 Other than a loan covered by sub-para. (d) of the term "investment" in article 1138.

9 See the wording of article 1138, investment clause (j).

10 This is not defined by the agreement and may create interesting threshold issues due to its highly subjective nature.

11 The investment exception is at article 1101(3) and the financial service incorporation is at article 1401(2).

12 NAFTA annex III, Schedule of Mexico, at III-M-1 to III-M-4. All annex references to page numbers refer to the final version of the NAFTA.

13 For a discussion on the difference between bound and unbound reservations, see chapter 21 of this book.

2. INVESTMENT OBLIGATIONS

The Investment chapter contains four general NAFTA obligations which Parties are required to observe. These are national treatment, Most-Favoured-Nation status, limitations on investment restrictions and minimum standards for governmental behaviour on transfers and expropriation.

(a) NATIONAL TREATMENT

National treatment obligations are the trade law equivalents of the biblical golden rule "do onto others as you would have them do unto you"[14]. NAFTA Parties are obliged to give the investors of other NAFTA Parties treatment no less favourable then they give their own domestic investors. This commitment must be granted in connection with a list of specified basic corporate operations[15]. This national treatment obligation is similar to the pre-existing obligation of the three NAFTA countries under GATT Article III regarding goods.

(b) MOST-FAVOURED-NATION TREATMENT

NAFTA obligates its Parties to provide Most-Favoured-Nation (MFN) treatment[16]. When combined, NAFTA's national treatment and MFN requirements create a powerful obligation on governments to provide to NAFTA investors the best type of treatment they would provide to any investor, whether domestic or foreign.

Since the NAFTA deals with more than one level of government within each Party, the Agreement requires that subnational governments must provide the best "in-province" or "in-state" treatment available[17].

(c) SENIOR MANAGEMENT

The NAFTA contains a number of provisions which set out limitations on the ability of governments to restrict foreign investment. The NAFTA's provisions on performance requirements, senior management and expropriation touch on sensitive domestic sovereignty issues in both Canada and Mexico. Their inclusion in the NAFTA establishes a clear commitment from all three NAFTA Parties to a reduction in government intervention in investment issues.

---

14 Matthew 7:12.
15 NAFTA article 1102 lists these as establishment, acquisition, expansion, management, conduct, operation, and sale or other disposition of investments.
16 NAFTA article 1103.
17 NAFTA article 1102(3).

The NAFTA does not end government requirements that a certain percentage of corporate directors be nationals. What it does provide is limits on such government regulations. For example, regulations may specify that a majority of corporate directors be of a particular nationality, or residents, as long as the requirement "does not materially impair the ability of the investor to exercise control of its investment"[18]. Thus, federally incorporated businesses in Canada will still be required to have a majority of Canadian residents on the board of directors[19]. The NAFTA has a more restrictive effect on the senior management of state enterprises. NAFTA article 1107(1) prohibits government requirements that senior management of a state enterprise be of any particular nationality.

Canada has also included a reservation which permits it to require that the senior management and directors of Canadian crown corporations which are subsequently privatized, may be exempted from this NAFTA requirement[20].

(d) PERFORMANCE REQUIREMENTS

The NAFTA includes detailed provisions which restrict the imposition of performance requirements on investment by all levels of government. The intent of these provisions is to reduce the ability of government to require that businesses conform to these measures when investing in a Party. The obligations dealt with in the NAFTA go further than any similar obligations in the Canada-U.S. Free Trade Agreement[21] or the Uruguay Round GATT Agreement on Trade Related Investment Measures (TRIMs)[22]. The NAFTA imposes these obligations not only on the activity of NAFTA governments among themselves, but more generally by requiring this treatment of NAFTA governments concerning all countries.

The NAFTA's restrictions on investment-related performance requirements apply not only to the national level of government, but also extends to subnational governments as well[23]. The Agreement addresses performance requirements in two situations: those based on being in the market and those based on receiving some form of government advantage.

---

18 NAFTA article 1107(2). This addition may eventually be the subject of an interesting NAFTA decision on what constitutes the "material" impairment of control.

19 *Canada Business Corporations Act*, R.S.C. 1985, c. C-44, s. 105(3).

20 NAFTA annex I, Schedule of Canada, at I-C-7.

21 Canada-U.S. Free Trade Agreement article 1603.

22 The obligations in the TRIMs agreement cover a smaller range of performance requirements than does the NAFTA. The TRIMs code also does not apply to services at all unlike a number of the specific performance requirements contained in the NAFTA.

23 NAFTA article 1101(1)(c).

Certain performance requirements in relation to general corporate functions (the establishment, acquisition, expansion, management, conduct or operation of an investment) are prohibited by the NAFTA[24]. These obligations relate to investments of NAFTA Parties and non-parties alike. This provision is well-summarized in the American *Statement of Administrative Action* which states:

> Under Article 1106, a government may not, as a condition for the establishment or operation of an investment, require a firm to:
>
> • limit its sales in the domestic market by conditioning such sales on exports or foreign exchange earnings;
>
> • buy or use components from a local supplier or accord a preference to domestic goods or services[25];
>
> • achieve a minimum level of "domestic content";
>
> • limit its imports to a certain percentage of exports or foreign exchange inflows associated with the investment;
>
> • transfer technology to any domestic entity, except to remedy an alleged violation of competition law;
>
> • export a specified level of goods or services; or
>
> • supply designated regional or world markets solely from its local production[26].

The NAFTA constrains the power of governments to require certain performance requirements from being imposed as a condition for the receipt of a subsidy or other advantage such as a tax holiday[27]. The list is identical to that set out in article 1106(1) except for three modifications:

(a) there is no prohibition on requirements requiring the export of a given level of goods or services;

(b) there is no prohibition on performance measures related to the mandatory purchase of, or the giving of a preference to, local service providers; and

(c) there is no prohibition on requirements that an investment transfer technology to any domestic entity.

Many tools of government industrial policy are based on requiring businesses to follow certain behaviours as a condition for receiving government benefits. The NAFTA imposes some limits on these types of

---

24 NAFTA article 1106(1).
25 This could prohibit the requirement that only nationals be hired to work at an investment.
26 *Statement of Administrative Action* at 141.
27 NAFTA article 1106(3).

policies. However, the prohibition on performance requirements which are given in connection with subsidies is lessened to some extent by allowing Parties to make the receipt of a subsidy conditional with a list of requirements including: locating production, providing a service, training or employing workers, constructing or expanding particular facilities, or carrying out research and development[28].

Generally, the NAFTA performance requirement obligations will not restrict a Party from engaging in government procurement policies, subsidies, export promotion or foreign aid activities[29]. Canada has retained the right to require technology transfer in connection with reviews by Investment Canada, the Canadian foreign investment review agency[30]. Mexico has retained the right to maintain certain performance requirements in connection with its cultural and automotive industries[31].

One question which is left unanswered by article 1106 is the inter-relationship between the two types of situations envisioned by clauses (1) and (3). While the NAFTA states that the performance requirements listed in these two clauses are exhaustive[32], it does not give any textual support on how they are to be interpreted between themselves.

Article 1106 is written in a way which would provide clarity if the performance requirements imposed in connection with any one of the six listed corporate functions in clause (1) occurred at a different time than when an investment receives an advantage. Unfortunately, this situation is unlikely. Government advantages will necessarily be imposed in connection with the conduct or management of an investment's operations. In other words, the situation envisioned in clause (1) will always occur in situations envisioned in clause (3). Thus, one should expect to find a clause in this article which would govern the relationship between these two clauses, yet no such clause exists.

When the obligations of clause (1) are not inconsistent with the terms of clause (3), then both clauses will be able to operate freely. While article 1106(3) does not prohibit a government requirement that an investment use a certain level of domestic services if it receives a subsidy, article 1106(1)(a) would prohibit this from occurring. In such a situation, this performance requirement could not be imposed without offending the obligation in article 1106(1).

---

28 NAFTA article 1106(4).
29 NAFTA article 1108(8)(a)-(c).
30 NAFTA annex I, Schedule of Canada at I-C-2.
31 The cultural industry reservations are in NAFTA annex I, Schedule of Mexico from I-M-10 to I-M-14. The automotive reservations are in annex I, Schedule of Mexico from I-M-32 to I-M-38.
32 NAFTA article 1106(5).

Because of the important nature of the government policies being disciplined by article 1106, this ambiguity could lead to a dispute between the NAFTA Parties or the filing of an investor-state dispute. There is significant support for the view that the broader obligations of article 1106(1) will apply to every investment-performance requirement situation unless there is a direct conflict between the two provisions. An authoritative decision on the relationship between these clauses remains elusive and will likely only be resolved through the decision of a NAFTA dispute panel[33].

(e) MINIMUM TREATMENT, EXPROPRIATION AND TRANSFERS

The NAFTA provisions dealing with minimum treatment, expropriation and transfers constitute a clear advantage for the developed economies of the new trilateral trading region. The NAFTA marks the first occasion where a Latin American country has freely assented to an international obligation, which could be taken to an international arbitral body, requiring foreign companies to be treated in the same way as domestic ones during expropriation. In effect, in assenting to the NAFTA, Mexico has distanced itself from its regional approach, known as the Calvo clause[34].

The NAFTA Parties have guaranteed that they will treat the investments of the other Parties in accordance with international legal concepts of minimum acceptable treatment. This concept has been fortified with specific commitments regarding fair treatment in the event of expropriation. The obligations speak to more than simple expropriation, for the terms of article 1110 speak to expropriation or "acts tantamount to expropriation". The NAFTA does not include any definition of what constitutes an act tantamount to expropriation. This is an area which is certain to receive attention from future NAFTA dispute settlement panels as acts which are not considered to constitute expropriation by the host state, but which impair the benefits of NAFTA investors, may be subject to this NAFTA obligation.

The NAFTA imposes obligations on the handling of expropriation. Expropriation may only occur under certain circumstances: it may only take place for a public purpose, on a non-discriminatory basis and in accordance with principles of due process of law. Parties must provide compensation without unreasonable delay at market value but these concepts of delay and

---

33 In this situation, it is likely that the more specific wording of article 1106(3) would likely be relied upon, but this would be a decision left up to an eventual arbitrator.

34 The Calvo clause is named for the Argentinean jurist who first wrote it. It provides that foreign investors agree to waive the diplomatic protection of their home state and that they will abide by the decisions of local courts for all contractual disputes.

market value have not been defined by the Agreement. There are no reservations allowed in the NAFTA to these commitments, not for national governments, not for subnational, nor even local governments. All levels of government are bound by this commitment.

NAFTA article 1109 provides that NAFTA investors will be able to freely transfer local funds relating to an investment of a NAFTA investor. Parties must allow currency at market rates to be transferred for the earnings, dividends, fees and proceeds of the investments of NAFTA investors from other Parties. This provision also guarantees that businesses will be able to transfer funds to be able to pay principal and interest on loans or for their subsidiaries to pay third parties. This is a critical provision for it guarantees that NAFTA investors will be able to freely buy and sell local currency and be able to repatriate their profits.

3. GOVERNMENT SOCIAL SERVICES AND THE INVESTMENT CHAPTER

Trade disputes between Canada and the United States on issues such as softwood lumber have identified that there can be significant differences in view as to what constitutes the appropriate role for government action. Nowhere is this debate more clearly caught by the NAFTA than when examining the relationship between social services and the Investment chapter.

Article 1101(4) purports to exempt governments from the NAFTA's investment obligations for law enforcement, corrections and certain social services. The provision reads as follows:

> Nothing in this Chapter shall be construed to prevent a Party from providing a service or performing a function such as law enforcement, correctional services, income security or insurance, social security or insurance, social welfare, public education, public training, health, and child care, in a manner that is not inconsistent with this Chapter.

While this section would appear to allow governments to continue these listed services, the addition of the words "in a manner that is not inconsistent with this Chapter" entirely removes the effect of the exception. The value of an exception is where it speaks to items which are otherwise inconsistent with the Agreement. Thus, the article 1101(4) exception must be considered to be a diplomatic statement rather than a legal one.

It should be noted that Canada, Mexico and the United States have made virtually identical reservations on this subject in annex II[35]. These reservations read that the government:

---

35 The Canadian reservation is at NAFTA annex II, Schedule of Canada at II-C-9, the

reserves the right to adopt or maintain any measure with respect to the provision of public law enforcement and correctional services, and the following services to the extent that they are social services established or maintained for a public purpose: income security or insurance, social security or insurance, social welfare, public education, public training, health, and child care.

The wording of this reservation provides more protection to government social programs than the article 1101(4) exception clause. However, it, too, raises questions. For example, the provisions to which this reservation applies are narrow[36]. In addition, the annex establishes two categories of services. Government measures regarding law enforcement and correctional services are totally reserved. Questions arise when one looks at the other government social services. Programs such as government-sponsored health care or workers compensation would only be reserved "to the extent that they are social services established or maintained for a public purpose". This wording certainly raises ambiguity. The meaning of this wording, and thus the effect of this part of the reservation will inevitably be determined by the NAFTA Free Trade Commission or a chapter 20 panel[37].

4. SPECIAL TREATMENT FOR FOREIGN INVESTMENT REVIEW

During the negotiations of the Canada-U.S. Free Trade Agreement, there was significant attention paid to the issue of reducing the scope of foreign investment review by the Canadian government. Before 1984, Canada reviewed all new foreign investment under the *Foreign Investment Review Act*. This Act provided substantial review of new investment in Canada by foreigners. The election of a Conservative government to the Canadian Parliament in 1984 resulted in the amendment of the *Foreign Investment Review Act* by the *Investment Canada Act*. Under the *Investment Canada Act*, only direct acquisitions valued at over CDN $5 million and CDN $50 million in indirect ones were reviewable[38].

It had been a longstanding goal of American trade policy to reduce impediments to American investment abroad such as the *Foreign Investment Review Act*. Under the Canada-U.S. Free Trade Agreement, Canada agreed to grant special treatment to American investment in Canada. That

---

Mexican reservation is at NAFTA annex II, Schedule of Mexico at II-M-11 and the American is at NAFTA annex II, Schedule of the United States at II-U-5.

36 These reservations only apply to the investment chapter's obligations regarding national treatment, and rules regarding senior management and boards of directors.

37 NAFTA article 1132 provides that the Free Trade Commission will provide binding interpretation of annexes for investor-state disputes. Otherwise, in state-to-state disputes, the chapter 20 procedures will apply.

38 Acquisitions in the cultural industries area may also be reviewed.

agreement's annex 1607.3 reduced the scope for foreign investment review by Canada of American investment only to direct acquisitions over CDN $150 million. Review of indirect acquisitions was phased out entirely[39].

The desire to remove impediments to foreign investment was raised again during the NAFTA negotiations with a special focus on the extensive Mexican foreign investment review process. In Mexico, as in Canada, the issue of foreign investment review was politically charged. Mexico differed from Canada in having obligations regarding foreign investment entrenched specifically in its national constitution[40] and deeply rooted in its national psyche.

The NAFTA provides that Mexico may review foreign investments by NAFTA investors over US $25 million phased for the first 10 years of the Agreement's operation. Canada simply maintained its ability to review foreign investments as set out in the Canada-U.S. Free Trade Agreement[41]. Within NAFTA annex III, Mexico reserved areas such as ownership restrictions for its petrochemical industry pursuant to the Mexican Constitution. Measures allowing for government review of foreign investment were reserved by both Mexico and Canada.

---

39 Canada maintained its ability to review all investment in cultural industries.
40 This issue as it relates to provisions prohibiting foreign investment in the energy sector is discussed in chapter 6.
41 NAFTA annex I, Schedule of Canada at I-C-2.

12

Cross-Border Trade in Services

In her excellent book which gives some context and understanding to the new economy in Canada and the United States, economist Nuala Beck has identified that nearly all of the "engines" of the new economy are based within the services sector[1].

The creation of a comprehensive agreement governing trade in services was a key goal for the NAFTA negotiators. Both the U.S.-Israel Free Trade Agreement and the Canada-U.S. Free Trade Agreement contained limited provisions regarding trade in services[2]. The NAFTA followed this precedent to create extensive disciplines on government activity regarding services. The NAFTA cross-border trade in services provisions establish a set of basic rules and obligations which facilitate trade in services among its Parties. The NAFTA also demonstrates some thematic similarity to the Uruguay Round General Agreement on Trade in Services (GATS), but there are some differences between these agreements[3].

1. SCOPE OF THE SERVICES CHAPTER

The NAFTA Services chapter applies to measures taken by a Party regarding the cross-border trade in services by service providers of another Party, including[4]:

(a) the production, distribution, marketing, sale and delivery of a service;

(b) the purchase or use of, or payment for a service;

(c) the access to, and use of distribution and transportation systems in connection with the provision of a service;

---

1 Nuala Beck, *Shifting Gears: Thriving in the New Economy.* (Toronto: Harper Collins Publishers, 1992).

2 U.S.-Israel Free Trade Agreement, Jan. 1, 1985, 24 I.L.M. 301. The U.S.-Israel Agreement only contained a commitment to take best efforts to abide by the agreement's principles. The Canada-U.S. Free Trade Agreement contained a chapter on cross-border trade in services but its scope was much more limited than the NAFTA's.

3 For example, the NAFTA provides a two-year period for subnational governments to list reservations, while the GATS provides no advance period for the listing of reservations.

4 NAFTA article 1201(1).

(d) the presence in its territory of a service provider of another Party; and
(e) the provision of a bond or other form of financial security as a condition for the provision of a service.

The services listed in article 1201 do not comprise an exhaustive list of covered services but, are merely examples of covered cross-border services. Thus, this chapter covers the broad range of service industries with the exception of financial services and telecommunications, both of which are specifically addressed within their own NAFTA chapters[5].

There are some limits on the scope of the Services chapter. It does not apply to issues such as air services[6], government procurement[7] or government subsidies[8]. As with the Investment chapter obligations, Parties have a right to make "bound" reservations for themselves and for their subnational governments. Reservations for measures at the federal level were contained in the NAFTA. Reservations for subnationals may only be taken for non-conforming measures that were in existence on January 1, 1994, and may only be taken by January 1, 1996. Measures by local governments are not affected by the NAFTA at all. Each NAFTA Party has also made general "unbound reservations" in NAFTA annex II. These unbound reservations allow new measures to be taken in these specific areas unimpeded by NAFTA obligations. These reservations include the maritime industry[9] (other than some services between Canada and Mexico) and matters entrenched in the Mexican Constitution as being restricted to the government of Mexico and its nationals[10].

2. CROSS-BORDER SERVICE OBLIGATIONS

Like the NAFTA Investment chapter, the Services chapter establishes a general set of obligations upon governments. These obligations require national treatment, Most-Favoured-Nation treatment, an end to local presence requirements and new requirements on licensing requirements.

---

5 Financial services are addressed in NAFTA chapter 14 and telecommunications services in chapter 13.
6 Air services are covered by bilateral agreements. Specialty air services, such as surveying, aircraft repair and aircraft maintenance are covered by the NAFTA.
7 Government procurement of services is covered exclusively by NAFTA chapter 10.
8 NAFTA article 1201(2).
9 NAFTA annex I, Schedule of Canada at II-C-13, NAFTA annex II, Schedule of the United States at II-U-10.
10 NAFTA annex II, Schedule of Mexico at II-M-2 to II-M-9 and II-M-11 to II-M-12.

(a) NATIONAL TREATMENT

Each NAFTA Party is obligated to treat service providers of other NAFTA Parties no less favourably than it treats its own service providers[11]. With respect to measures of a state or province, national treatment means treatment no less favourable than the most favourable treatment that the subnational accords to the service providers of the country of which it forms a part[12].

(b) MOST-FAVOURED-NATION TREATMENT

The NAFTA Services chapter requires that Parties provide Most-Favoured-Nation treatment to the service providers of other NAFTA Parties in its territory. Thus service providers of the other NAFTA Parties may be treated no less favourably than service providers of any other country in similar circumstances. Furthermore, if there is any difference in the level of service to be given, Parties are required to give the better of national treatment or Most-Favoured-Nation treatment to the service providers of other Parties[13].

(c) LOCAL PRESENCE

The NAFTA prohibits governments from requiring service providers to establish a presence (such as an office) within the territory of a NAFTA Party as a condition of market access[14]. This condition will have the effect of removing a large number of regulatory measures which required service providers to have a local office as a means of assuring consumer protection. Other means such as bonding requirements will have to suffice for such measures in future.

(d) QUANTITATIVE RESTRICTIONS

NAFTA Parties are able to maintain existing non-discriminatory measures that limit the number of service providers, or the operations of service providers, in a particular sector. These measures maintained at the federal level were listed in NAFTA annex V before January 1, 1994. State and provincial measures must be listed in the same annex by January 1, 1995 but local measures need not be listed.[15] The purpose of listing these

---

11 NAFTA article 1202.
12 NAFTA article 1202(2).
13 NAFTA article 1204.
14 NAFTA article 1205.
15 NAFTA article 1207.

measures is to identify what constitutes the quantitative trade restrictive measures of the NAFTA Parties. This annex will become the basis for future liberalization discussions between the Parties[16].

(e) DENIAL OF BENEFITS

A NAFTA Party is entitled to deny the benefits of the Services chapter to a service provider if the services involved are provided through an enterprise of another NAFTA Party that is owned or controlled by persons of a non-NAFTA country and that enterprise has no substantive business activities in the NAFTA territory[17]. In the area of transportation services, a NAFTA Party may deny benefits to a firm if these services are provided with equipment that is registered in a non-NAFTA country[18].

(f) LICENSING

The NAFTA contains provisions related to professional licensing and certification which are designed to reduce barriers to trade. Specifically, each Party will endeavour to ensure that its licensing and certification requirements and procedures are:[19]

- based on objective and transparent criteria such as professional competence;
- no more burdensome than is necessary to ensure the quality of the service; and
- not a disguised restriction on the cross-border provision of the service.

While the NAFTA provides a mechanism for the reciprocal recognition of licenses and certifications, reciprocal recognition is not obligatory[20]. By January 1, 1996, the NAFTA Parties are obligated to remove citizenship or residency requirements for the licensing and certification of professional service providers in its territory that are listed in its NAFTA reservations[21]. However, the failure to comply with this obligation will only allow the other Parties to maintain reciprocal requirements in that sector. Professional licensing issues are more fully developed in a sectoral annex contained at the end of the Services chapter.

---

16 NAFTA article 1207(4).
17 NAFTA article 1211(2).
18 NAFTA article 1211(1)(b).
19 NAFTA article 1210.
20 NAFTA article 1210(2).
21 NAFTA article 1210(3).

(g) PROFESSIONAL SERVICES

One of the most pervasive non-tariff barriers to free trade in services has been the inability to establish internationally-acceptable professional standards. Indeed, there is even a lack of free trade within the NAFTA countries on this issue. Qualified professionals, such as medical doctors, may not practice in many states or provinces without passing a number of time-consuming examinations.

The difficulty of establishing professional recognition has shown itself in other international agreements. Establishing a method for the recognition of professional criteria was a time consuming and complex task for the European Union, which has full labour mobility as one of its essential terms[22]. The NAFTA does not nearly go as far as the European Union; the NAFTA does not provide for full labour mobility nor for professional service mobility.

NAFTA annex 1210.5 provides a commitment by the NAFTA Parties to encourage professional bodies in each NAFTA Party to develop mutually acceptable standards for licensing professionals and reciprocal recognition[23]. There is no time limit on this process under the NAFTA. The decision on recognition and standards is entirely up to the professional bodies. The NAFTA does not impose any standards or commitments other than to require Parties to fairly review and answer applications by NAFTA Party nationals for professional licensing[24].

While the NAFTA does not require recognition of foreign lawyers, it does provide a special section for foreign legal consultants; lawyers who are licensed in another jurisdiction and wish to give advice on their own law in another NAFTA Party. For example, Canada will allow foreign legal consultants to provide services in Ontario, British Columbia and Saskatchewan[25]. Mexico and 15 American jurisdictions will permit lawyers authorized to practice in other NAFTA jurisdictions, to provide foreign legal consultants in their jurisdictions[26]. The NAFTA Parties have also undertaken commitments to develop licensing standards for professional engineers.

---

22 For more on this, see Derrick Wyatt and Alan Dashwood, *The Substantive Law of the EEC*, 2nd ed.(London: Sweet & Maxwell, 1987) at 210-213.
23 NAFTA annex 1210.5(2).
24 NAFTA annex 1210.5(1).
25 NAFTA annex VI, Schedule of Canada, at VI-C-1.
26 Mexico has provided for this at annex VI, Schedule of Mexico at VI-M-2. The United States has provided its commitment at annex VI, Schedule of the United States at VI-U-2.

3. TRANSPORTATION

An annex to the Services chapter deals exclusively with land transportation between the NAFTA Parties. Other than the area of cabotage[27], the land transportation annex deals with all areas of land transportation between the Parties. Prior to the NAFTA, the United States imposed a moratorium[28] against the new grant of operating authority to Mexican bus and truck carriers[29]. This moratorium was lifted against Canadian truck and bus carriers in 1982[30]. Land transportation will have gradual liberalizations on the following schedule:

January 1, 1994	The United States will grant Mexican charter and tour buses access[31].
December 17, 1995	The United States will allow Mexican truckers to gain access to American border states[32] and may establish companies to distribute international cargo in the United States[33]. Mexican companies will be entitled to pick up and deliver cargo directly from the United States to Mexico[34]. Mexico will allow NAFTA investors to acquire up to 49 percent of bus companies and truck carriers which provide international cargo services[35]. Permissable ownership levels will increase to 51 percent after January 1, 2001. All limits will be abolished on January 1, 2004[36].
January 1, 1997	The United States will permit Mexican-scheduled bus companies to serve the United States market[37]. Mexico will grant reciprocal status to the other NAFTA Parties[38].

---

27 Cabotage is the point-to-point domestic carriage of cargo.
28 The *Bus Regulatory Reform Act* of 1982, 49 U.S.C. §10927.
29 NAFTA annex I, Schedule of the United States, cross-border (1) at I-U-19.
30 *Statement of Government Action* at 158.
31 NAFTA annex I, Schedule of the United States, cross-border (2) at I-U-19.
32 These border states are California, Arizona, New Mexico and Texas. NAFTA annex I - Schedule of the United States, cross-border (a) at I-U-20.
33 NAFTA annex I, Schedule of the United States, investment (a) at I-U-20.
34 The border states are Baja California, Chihuahua, Coahuila, Nuevo León, Sonora and Tamaulipas. NAFTA annex I, Schedule of Mexico, cross-border (a) at I-M-69.
35 NAFTA annex I, Schedule of Mexico, investment (a) at I-M-63.
36 NAFTA annex I, Schedule of Mexico, investment (b) and (c) at I-M-63.
37 NAFTA annex I, Schedule of the United States, cross-border (b) at I-U-20.
38 NAFTA annex I, Schedule of Mexico, cross-border (b) at I-M-70.

January 1, 2000   The United States will allow unrestricted Mexican truck services throughout its territory[39]. Mexico will provide the same access to the other NAFTA Parties[40].

An annex to the NAFTA Technical Barriers to Trade chapter establishes a Land Transportation Standards Subcommittee to review standards for bus, truck and rail standards[41]. The subcommittee will attempt to make the standards-related measures of the NAFTA Parties compatible regarding the following:

- the non-medical testing and licensing of truck drivers within two and a half years[42];

- medical standards for truck drivers[43];

- vehicles, including measures such as tires and brakes, securement of cargo, weights and dimensions, maintenance and repair and emission levels, within three years[44];

- railway locomotives, other rail equipment and operating personnel standards relevant to cross-border operations[45];

- the transportation of dangerous goods[46]; and

- road signs and supervision of motor carrier safety compliance[47].

4. REVIEW PROCESS

Commencing on January 1, 1999, the Free Trade Commission will review the progress of liberalizations in the land transportation sector[48]. No later than January 1, 2001, the Parties will consult on further liberalization commitments[49].

---

39 NAFTA annex I, Schedule of the United States, cross-border (c) at I-U-20.
40 NAFTA annex I, Schedule of Mexico, cross-border (c) at I-M-70.
41 NAFTA annex 913.5.a-1.
42 NAFTA annex 913.5.a-1(2)(a)(i).
43 NAFTA annex 913.5.a-1(2)(a)(ii).
44 NAFTA annex 913.5.a-1(2)(a)(iii).
45 NAFTA annex 913.5.a-1(2)(b)(i).
46 NAFTA annex 913.5.a-1(2)(c).
47 NAFTA annex 913.5.a-1(2)(a)(v).
48 NAFTA annex 1212(2).
49 NAFTA annex 1212(3).

13

Telecommunications

The NAFTA recognizes the centrality of telecommunications services in the contemporary global economy. Access to networks for the transfer of voice and electronic data have become critical corporate needs. The NAFTA has devoted an entire chapter to trade in telecommunications services which augments its general investment and cross-border service commitments contained in other chapters[1]. The NAFTA provisions in this chapter mark an expansion on the telecommunications commitments contained in the Canada-U.S. Free Trade Agreement[2]. They also contain many similar commitments to the Telecommunications Annex contained in the Uruguay Round General Agreement on Trade in Services.

1. SCOPE OF THE TELECOMMUNICATIONS CHAPTER

NAFTA article 1301 establishes that the Telecommunications chapter applies to:

(a) measures relating to access and use of public telecommunications transport networks or services by persons of another Party;

(b) measures relating to the provision of enhanced or value-added services by persons of another Party; and

(c) standards measures relating to attachment of terminal or other equipment to public telecommunications transport networks.

This chapter has a significant restriction in that the operation and provision of public networks and basic communications services are not included in the chapter's coverage. However, reasonable access to the public network is an important part of the Telecommunications chapter's obligations. In addition, the distribution of radio or television programming by stations or cable systems is exempt from the chapter's obligations[3].

---

1 NAFTA article 1307 provides that in the event of a conflict between the provisions of the Telecommunications chapter and any other NAFTA provision, the Telecommunications chapter provision will prevail to the extent of the inconsistency.

2 Canada-U.S. Free Trade Agreement annex 1404-C.

3 NAFTA article 1301(3)(c) and (d).

2. TELECOMMUNICATIONS OBLIGATIONS

This chapter contains four basic obligations which provide certainty in the provision of telecommunications services within each NAFTA Party.

(a) ACCESS

The telecommunications access obligation is a modification of the national treatment obligation provided elsewhere in the NAFTA. In this chapter, the NAFTA provides that public telecommunications transport networks and services are to be made available, on reasonable and non-discriminatory terms for certain uses, to firms or individuals from other NAFTA Parties[4]. These uses include the provision of enhanced or value-added telecommunications services and intra-corporate communications. The term "non-discriminatory" in this context is defined to mean access provided on terms and conditions no less favourable than those accorded to any other customer or user of similar public telecommunications transport networks or services in similar circumstances[5].

(b) PROVISION OF ENHANCED SERVICES

Parties are committed to provide licensing or other authorization procedures for the provision of enhanced or value-added telecommunications services in a manner which is transparent, non-discriminatory and applied expeditiously. Enhanced telecommuncations providers of the three countries will not be subject to obligations that are normally imposed on providers of public networks and services, such as providing services to the public generally or cost-justifying their rates[6]. The NAFTA removes restrictions on investment in value-added telecommunications services in Mexico except for video-text and enhanced packet switching services[7]. Investment restrictions on the remaining services will end on July 1, 1995[8].

NAFTA obligates Parties to undertake pricing decisions for access to NAFTA Party businesses based on the economic costs of accessing the system[9]. Conditions on access and use may be imposed only when necessary to safeguard the public service responsibilities of network operators or to protect the technical integrity of public networks[10].

---

4 NAFTA article 1302.
5 NAFTA article 1302(8).
6 NAFTA article 1303(2).
7 NAFTA annex I, Schedule of Mexico, investment (4) at I-M-19.
8 NAFTA annex I, Schedule of Mexico, phase-out: investment at I-M-19.
9 NAFTA article 1303(3)(a).
10 NAFTA article 1302(6).

(c) STANDARDS-RELATED MEASURES

The use of technical standards as a barrier to access has been strictly regulated by the NAFTA[11]. The NAFTA limits the types of standards-related measures that may be imposed on the attachment of telecommunications equipment to public networks. Such measures must be necessary to prevent technical damage to, and interference with, public networks and services, to prevent billing equipment malfunctions and to ensure user safety and access[12]. Conformity assessment procedures on telecommunication equipment must be based on non-discrimination and transparency[13]. By January 1, 1995, each Party is required to accept the equipment test results conducted by other NAFTA Parties[14]. This obligation supplements the obligation of the Telecommunications Standards Subcommittee[15] which will develop a timetable for standards-related measures for telecommunications equipment[16].

In addition, any technically-qualified entity will be permitted to test equipment to be attached to public networks. This section also establishes procedures in each country that permit the acceptance of equipment test results conducted in the other NAFTA countries.

(d) MONOPOLIES

The NAFTA requires that monopoly providers of basic telecommunications services may not engage in anticompetitive practices that would adversely affect a person from another Party[17]. This requirement augments other NAFTA regulations affecting monopolies contained in NAFTA's chapter 15.

(e) TECHNICAL COOPERATION

The NAFTA Parties are obliged to cooperate in the exchange of technical information and in the development of government-to-government training programs[18]. The Parties will also promote standards through the International Telecommunications Union and the International Organi-

---

11 Standards regulation obligations occur primarily in chapters 7 and 9.
12 NAFTA article 1304(1).
13 NAFTA article 1304(5).
14 NAFTA article 1304(6).
15 NAFTA article 913(5)(a)(ii) created this body.
16 NAFTA annex 913.5.a-2(2).
17 NAFTA article 1305(1).
18 NAFTA article 1309.

zation for Standardization[19]. The Telecommunications Standards Subcommittee may also consider whatever telecommunications matters that it deems appropriate[20].

---

19 NAFTA article 1308.
20 NAFTA annex 913.51-2(4).

14

Financial Services

Like the Investment and Services chapters, the NAFTA's Financial Services chapter can trace its roots back to the Canada-U.S. Free Trade Agreement. Chapter 17 of that agreement established liberalized cross-border trade in financial services between Canada and the United States in a limited number of areas. The NAFTA Financial Services chapter expands upon this foundation by applying its commitments to all financial institutions and services in Canada, Mexico and the United States. The chapter also contains a list of specific financial service commitments from each NAFTA Party.

1. SCOPE OF THE FINANCIAL SERVICES CHAPTER

Article 1401(1) provides that the NAFTA applies to all measures[1] adopted or maintained by a Party relating to the:

(a) financial institutions of another Party;
(b) investors of another Party, and the investments of such investors, in financial institutions in the Party's territory; and
(c) cross-border trade in financial services.

The Agreement defines a financial institution as being a "financial intermediary or other enterprise" that is authorized to do business and supervised as a financial institution under the law of the host Party[2]. As a result, the NAFTA Financial Services chapter applies broadly to insurance, securities and banking services. In addition, while the Canada-U.S. Free Trade Agreement exempted subnationals from coverage[3], the NAFTA covers all measures taken by the Party, including those measures taken by subnational governments and certain self-regulatory organizations. The wording of the Financial Services chapter has left some ambiguities. For example, there appears to be some uncertainty about whether financial service businesses including mortgage brokers, insurance agents and bro-

---

1 The term measure is defined by NAFTA article 201 to include any law, regulation, procedure, requirement or practice.
2 NAFTA article 1416.
3 Canada-U.S. Free Trade Agreement article 1703(1).

kers who are principally regulated at the subnational level, are covered by this chapter or the Services chapter.

Parties have maintained the authority to exclusively conduct public retirement plans and statutory social security[4]. These schemes are not subject to the chapter's national treatment obligations[5]. Activities or services, guaranteed or financed by a Party, or its public entities, may be continued. Thus, for example, the provision of publicly-funded health plans is not affected by the provisions of this chapter even though there is a financial service component to these plans[6].

The scope of the Financial Services chapter has been enlarged by reading into it a number of obligations set out in other NAFTA chapters through article 1401(2). These provisions include the following:

- the right to transfer profits freely and without delay[7];
- the right to fair treatment on expropriation, or acts tantamount to expropriation[8];
- requirements regarding the imposition of special formalities[9];
- the ability to deny NAFTA benefits to non-NAFTA Party-controlled enterprises[10]; and
- the obligation to not lower standards in order to attract investment[11].

The chapter also provides for a very broad class of exceptions to its obligations. Parties are permitted to "adopt or maintain reasonable measures for prudential reasons"[12]. The NAFTA provides some examples of prudential reasons: the protection of investors or depositors, the maintenance of the integrity of financial institutions and ensuring the integrity of the Party's financial system. This listing of examples is not exhaustive.

The Canada-U.S. Free Trade Agreement did not contain any provision similar to the NAFTA prudential exception, however, the extent of the financial service obligations was substantially narrower in their earlier agreement. The original GATT failed to deal with the issue of financial services at all. The Uruguay Round General Agreement on Trade in Serv-

---

4 NAFTA article 1401(3).
5 NAFTA article 1410(3).
6 NAFTA article 1401(3)(b). It should be noted that article 1410(3) exempts s. 1401(3)(a) but not s. 1401(3)(b) from the national treatment obligation in chapter 14. Thus, governments which provide services using their own financial resources are required to apply national treatment and the other NAFTA financial service obligations.
7 NAFTA article 1109.
8 NAFTA article 1110.
9 NAFTA article 1111.
10 NAFTA articles 1113 and 1213.
11 NAFTA article 1114.
12 NAFTA article 1410.

ices (GATS) has a similar obligation. Article XIV of the GATS allows Parties to take actions otherwise inconsistent with the GATS if they are[13]:

(a) necessary to protect public morals or maintain public order;

(b) necessary to protect human, animal or plant life or health;

(c) necessary to secure compliance with laws or regulations which are not inconsistent with the provision of this Agreement including those relating to:

    i) the prevention of deceptive and fraudulent practices or to deal with the effects of a default on services contracts;

    ii) the protection of the privacy of individuals in relation to the processing and dissemination of personal data and the protection of confidentiality of individual records and accounts;

    iii) safety.

The GATS provides for limited exceptions for the types of policies permitted by the NAFTA prudential exception. For example, there is no clear exemption of governmental policies in the NAFTA for the purpose of protecting the financial integrity of the financial system by preventing deceptive practices.

While the NAFTA prudential exception appears broad, it too has its limits. All measures which governments seek to exempt from the NAFTA must be both reasonable and prudential[14]. These limits can be assessed by the Free Trade Commission during any investor-state dispute[15] and by a dispute settlement panel during a state-to-state dispute. These restrictions could limit the breadth of these exceptions in future.

Reservations by national and subnational governments to the financial service obligations may only be taken for non-conforming measures which were in existence on January 1, 1994. Parties were required to list their "bound" reservations for all Canadian provinces and six American states in annex VII by January 1, 1994[16]. While all national-level measures were listed by this date, it appears that the subnational lists of the United States and Canada were not listed by that date[17]. Thus, the validity of these subnational reservations is open to some question[18].

---

13 General Agreement on Trade in Services (GATS), 1994, Article XIV.

14 NAFTA article 1410(1).

15 NAFTA article 1415(2).

16 This requirement for all Canadian provinces and six American states is set out in annex 1409.1. Mexico is not required to list subnational reservations since all of its financial service regulation is carried out at the federal level.

17 *Inside NAFTA*, Jan. 12, 1994 at 1.

18 There is no provision within the NAFTA text which allows the Parties to extend the deadline for reservations. While the Parties agreed to the extension by an official exchange of letters, there is no ability to recognize this status under the NAFTA.

2. FINANCIAL SERVICE OBLIGATIONS

The Financial Services chapter contains general obligations for its Parties. These include special national treatment obligation, Most-Favoured-Nation treatment, rights of establishment and obligations regarding senior management and boards of directors. These general obligations are augmented by country-specific commitments.

(a) NATIONAL TREATMENT

NAFTA Parties are obliged to give the financial service providers of other NAFTA Parties treatment no less favourable then they give their own domestic providers in like circumstances[19]. NAFTA article 1405(5) adds an extra gloss to this obligation by adding an additional national treatment obligation for NAFTA Parties in the financial services area. This special obligation is known as equality of competitive opportunity (ECO). The ECO obligation establishes that measures which apply equally to domestic and foreign goods could still be discriminatory if they have the incidental effect of placing the foreign goods at a competitive disadvantage. This doctrine has been carried into the NAFTA from recent GATT jurisprudence[20]. The addition of this doctrine could result in significantly increased market access for NAFTA Party financial service providers.

NAFTA article 1405(5) appears to be based on the ECO obligation contained in Article XVII:3 of the GATS. However, it should be noted that there is a key difference between the NAFTA and the GATS commitments. The interpretive note to this GATS article states that[21]:

> Specific commitments assumed under this Article shall not be construed to require Parties to compensate for any inherent competitive disadvantage which results from the foreign character of the relevant service or service suppliers.

The purpose of this wording is to protect Parties from claims predicated upon the discriminatory structure of domestic service regimes. The NAFTA fails to provide similar protection to its governments. The only protection against claims made under the ECO obligation appears in NAFTA article

---

19 Article 1405.
20 For example in the GATT Panel Decision on s. 337 of the *U.S. Tariff Act of 1930* (adopted on Nov. 7, 1989, GATT L/6439), the panel stated at 51:
    The words "treatment no less favourable" in paragraph 4 (of GATT article III) call for effective equality of opportunities for imported products in respect of the application of laws, regulations and requirements affecting the internal sale, offering for sale, purchase, transportation, distribution or use of products. This clearly sets a minimum permissible standard.
21 GATS n. 11.

1405(7) which attempts to minimize the exposure of Parties to these types of challenges. It states:

> Differences in market share, profitability or size do not in themselves establish a denial of equal competitive opportunities, but such differences may be used as evidence regarding whether a Party's treatment affords equal competitive opportunities.

Nothing in this NAFTA article protects governments from claims of systemic competitive disadvantage. Accordingly, governments may well be liable to challenges based on the lost opportunity cost for foreign financial service providers who are unable to participate in financial service market access[22].

(b) MOST-FAVOURED-NATION TREATMENT

NAFTA Parties are obliged to provide treatment no less favourable to other NAFTA investors than it gives in like circumstances to the investors of any other country[23].

(c) RIGHTS OF ESTABLISHMENT[24]

Financial service providers of a Party may establish financial institutions in any other Party.

At the same time, each Party may require an investor to incorporate, under its domestic law, any financial institution that it establishes and it may impose terms and conditions which are consistent with the NAFTA's National Treatment obligation. This understanding falls short of the U.S. negotiating objective, which was to obtain from Canada and Mexico a commitment to allow U.S. banks to establish branches in their territory. As a concession to American desires, Canada and Mexico have agreed that if the government of the United States amends U.S. law and permits commercial banks to expand into substantially all of the United States market, Canada and Mexico will review the market access provisions of the NAFTA[25].

---

22 This could occur through a dispute raised on the nullification or impairment of NAFTA Financial Services chapter benefits which are incorporated into chapter 14 by article 1401(2).
23 NAFTA article 1406.
24 NAFTA article 1403.
25 This obligation was also contained in the Canada-U.S. Free Trade Agreement, article 1702(3).

(d) RIGHTS TO CROSS-BORDER TRADE[26]

NAFTA Parties must allow their residents to purchase financial services from another NAFTA Party. No new restrictions may be imposed on the cross-border provision of financial services in a sector, unless the country has reserved that sector in the NAFTA annex[27].

(e) NEW FINANCIAL SERVICES

Parties must permit the financial institutions of another Party to deliver new financial services throughout the territory of NAFTA Parties[28]. The Party where the service takes place has the right to determine how that new service will be delivered and regulated. The NAFTA also requires that the financial institutions of other Parties be permitted the right to transfer data, in electronic or other form, which is required in the course of that institution's ordinary business[29].

(f) SENIOR MANAGEMENT[30]

NAFTA Parties may not require that senior management or essential personnel be of any particular nationality[31]. The Agreement maintains regulations that specify that a majority of corporate directors, or committees of directors, be of a particular nationality or residence. These measures may not "materially impair the ability of the investor to exercise control of its investment"[32].

(g) TRANSPARENCY[33]

The NAFTA obliges its Parties to provide, to the extent practicable, an opportunity to comment on new measures of general application. NAFTA Parties must make available to interested persons their requirements for completing applications for entry into their financial service markets. They also establish obligations to keep applicants informed of the status of their

---

26 NAFTA article 1404.
27 For example, Canada has reserved its ability to deal with the United States on the cross-border exchange of securities. annex VII, Schedule of Canada, Part B, s. 1 at VII-C-2. The United States has reserved a reciprocal commitment, annex VII, Schedule of the United States, Part B, at VII-U-13.
28 NAFTA article 1407.
29 NAFTA article 1407(2).
30 NAFTA article 1408.
31 NAFTA article 1408.
32 NAFTA article 1408(2).
33 NAFTA article 1411.

application. Parties are required to make administrative determinations on a completed application within 120 days, where practicable.

3. COUNTRY-SPECIFIC COMMITMENTS

The NAFTA Financial Services chapter does not provide a comprehensive discipline for government regulation of financial services. The reason for this lack of a comprehensive system must be attributed to the different approaches taken by each Party to financial service regulations. The prudential measures exception provides an opportunity for Parties to maintain their regulatory diversity. The country-specific commitments provide another.

(a) CANADIAN COMMITMENTS

Most of Canada's country-specific commitments are related to its earlier Free Trade Agreement with the United States. The NAFTA incorporated the country-specific obligations of the Canada-U.S. Free Trade Agreement[34]. These commitments include the following:

- American investors will continue to be exempt from Canadian prohibitions against non-resident ownership of more than 10 percent of the outstanding shares of trust and insurance companies (but not Schedule 1 banks). They will also not be restricted by the aggregate ownership limits on non-residents from owning more than 25 percent of the shares of a trust, insurance company and generally a Canadian Chartered Bank.

- Americans will also remain exempt from the Canadian asset ceiling rules which limited the aggregate asset holdings of foreign banks to 12 percent of the banking sector[35].

- American investors will not be required to secure approval from the Canadian Minister of Finance as a condition for the opening of multiple branches in Canada.

- American subsidiaries of American banks were entitled to transfer loans to their parent companies only subject to prudential regulation.

Within the NAFTA, Canada has also extended those Canada-U.S. Free Trade Agreement commitments which limit foreign ownership of Cana-

---

34 NAFTA annex 1401.4.
35 This rule in contained in s. 422.3(2) of the *Bank Act*.

dian-controlled foreign institutions and which limit the holdings of domestic assets of foreign banks to Mexico[36].

It should be noted that by incorporating the commitments of the Canada-U.S. Free Trade Agreement into the NAFTA, Canada has limited the application of the commitments only to those areas of financial services regulated by the Canadian federal government. While substantial areas of financial services are regulated by the Canadian provinces, they were not subject to the commitments in the Canada-U.S. Free Trade Agreement.

(b) MEXICAN COMMITMENTS

The government of Mexico made a number of specific commitments under the NAFTA. Mexico will allow financial service providers incorporated in another Party to establish financial institutions in Mexico, subject to certain aggregate market capital restrictions for a six-year transitional period[37].

These limits are set out as follows[38]:

Institution	Aggregate Capitalization of All Firms
Commercial Banks	1.5%
Securities Firms	4.0%
Casualty Insurers	1.5%
Life and Health Insurers	1.5%

By January 1, 2000, all Mexican restrictions will be eliminated[39]. Thereafter, temporary safeguard provisions may be applicable in the banking and securities sectors and may be imposed for a further seven years. During the six-year transition period, Mexico will limit aggregate market capitalization of the entire market in the following way[40].

---

36 NAFTA annex VII(C), Schedule of Canada, at VII-C-4 contains the commitment. The *Statement of Government Action* at 177 indicates that Canada has amended its domestic laws to extend the national treatment obligations that Canada gave to the United States in their Free Trade Agreement to Mexico.

37 NAFTA annex VII(B), Schedule of Mexico, para. 2 at VII-M-13.

38 NAFTA annex VII, Schedule of Mexico, Schedule B, para. 2 at VII-M-13.

39 NAFTA annex VII(B), Schedule of Mexico, para. 5 at VII-M-14.

40 NAFTA annex VII(B), Schedule of Mexico, para. 5 at VII-M-14.

Institution	Initial % limit	Final % limit
Commercial Banks	8	15
Securities Firms	10	20
Factoring Companies	10	20
Leasing Companies	10	20

After the transition period, bank acquisitions will remain subject to reasonable prudential considerations and a four percent market share limit on the resulting institution[41].

Foreign insurers may establish Mexican affiliates. These affiliates will be subject to aggregate limits of six percent of market share, which will grow to a limit of 12 percent in 1999. These affiliates are subject to the market share limits set at one-and-a-half percent[42].

Insurance investors from other NAFTA Parties may elect to follow a different route by forging a joint venture with Mexican insurers. This will allow the joint ventures to increase their foreign equity participation in a series of tranches, starting at 30 percent in 1994, 45 percent by 1997, and 100 percent by the year 2000[43]. These joint ventures will not be subject to aggregate or individual market share limits. Foreign insurers may establish Mexican affiliates. These affiliates will be subject to aggregate limits of six percent of market share, which will grow to a limit of 12 percent in 1999. These affiliates are subject to the market share limits set at one-and-a-half percent[44].

Mexico has committed itself to provide national treatment to financial service providers of other Parties for the establishment of affiliates to provide consumer, commercial or mortgage lending or credit card services. However, during the six-year transition period, the aggregate assets of such subsidiaries may not exceed three percent of the sum of the aggregate assets of all banks in Mexico plus the aggregate assets of all types of limited-scope financial institutions in Mexico[45].These limits will not affect affiliates of

41 NAFTA annex VII(B), Schedule of Mexico, para. 13 at VII-M-17.
42 NAFTA annex VII(B), Schedule of Mexico, para. 6 at VII-M-15.
43 NAFTA annex VII(B), Schedule of Mexico, para. 7 at VII-M-16.
44 NAFTA annex VII(B), Schedule of Mexico, para. 6 at VII-M-15.
45 NAFTA annex VII(B), Schedule of Mexico, para. 8 at VII-M-16.

automotive companies with respect to the vehicles such companies produce[46].

(c) AMERICAN COMMITMENTS

Mexican financial groups that owned a Mexican bank with American operations at the time the NAFTA came into force may continue to operate securities firms in the United States for five years after the acquisition.

This only applies to banks operating in the American market on January 1, 1992 and to securities firms operating in the U.S. market since June 30, 1992[47]. The securities firm may not acquire other securities firms in the United States, and will be subject to nondiscriminatory restrictions on transactions between it and its affiliates[48].

---

46 NAFTA annex VII(B), Schedule of Mexico, para. 8 at VII-M-16.
47 NAFTA annex VII(C), Schedule of the United States at VII-U-14.
48 NAFTA annex VII(C), Schedule of the United States, para. (b) at VII-U-14.

15

Competition Policy, Monopolies and State Enterprises

Competition Policy seeks to protect the process of free and fair competition within the marketplace. To oversee the markets, governments review issues such as the acquisition of market power by individual enterprises and monitor practices which may lead to the restraint of trade or to the abuse of a dominant market position. While governments serve as the watchdogs of competition policy, they also can participate in anti-competitive practices through the use of monopolies and state-own enterprises. Thus, the NAFTA contains a short chapter which links competition policy to the inter-related issues of monopolies and state-enterprises.

1. COMPETITION POLICY

Through the NAFTA, its Parties have recognized the importance of a competition policy. To this end, they have committed to having measures against anti-competitive business practices[1]. The Parties have agreed to cooperate on the enforcement of competition law. This includes co-operation on issues such as mutual legal assistance, notification, consultation and the exchange of information regarding the enforcement of competition policies throughout the territory of the NAFTA Parties[2].

2. MONOPOLIES AND STATE ENTERPRISES

Monopolies have been used by each of the NAFTA Parties as a means of providing essential services to the public. The NAFTA allows Parties to maintain current monopolies and to designate new monopolies. Before a Party may designate a monopoly which could affect the interests of another Party, the designating Party must provide written notification to the other

---

1 NAFTA article 1501. Article 1501(3) states that the failure to meet this obligation cannot be the basis for any NAFTA dispute panel.
2 NAFTA article 1501(2).

Party. The designating Party also must endeavour to minimize or eliminate any nullification or impairment to the benefits of the other Party[3].

(a) MONOPOLIES

The NAFTA rules extend to current and future federal government-owned monopolies and any privately-owned monopoly that a federal government may designate in the future. They set out the following obligations:

- If the monopoly is exercising a delegated governmental authority in connection to the monopoly good, the monopoly must act in a manner consistent with the Party's NAFTA obligations[4]. This obligation can be enforced directly by investors through the NAFTA's investor-state dispute settlement process[5].

- When pricing, marketing, buying or selling a monopoly good or service, the NAFTA requires that the monopoly must "act solely in accordance with commercial considerations"[6]. This is defined to mean that the monopoly must take action consistent with normal business practices of privately-held enterprises[7].

- These monopolies are also obliged not to discriminate against the goods or businesses of the other Parties nor to engage in anti-competitive practices. Government-controlled monopolies may not use their positions to engage in anti-competitive practices in their territory[8].

These obligations do not apply to procurement by governments for their own use[9].

(b) STATE ENTERPRISES

GATT Article XVII deals with imports and exports of state trading enterprises. These bodies are required to abide by GATT principles of non-discrimination in the treatment of imports from other parties. The NAFTA broadens the GATT obligations by extending their scope to all state enterprises and by expanding the commitments of Parties.

---

3 NAFTA article 1502(2). The concept of nullification and impairment is reviewed in chapter 20 of this book.
4 NAFTA article 1502.
5 NAFTA article 1116(b).
6 NAFTA article 1502(3)(b).
7 NAFTA article 1505.
8 NAFTA article 1503.
9 NAFTA article 1502(4).

NAFTA article 1503 imposes obligations upon state enterprises at both the national and subnational level. These government-owned corporations must act in a manner that is consistent with the NAFTA's Investment and Financial Services chapters, wherever such an enterprise exercises a delegated governmental authority[10]. These enterprises are also required to provide non-discriminatory treatment to the goods or services of investors from other NAFTA Parties.

The definition of state enterprises differs for each NAFTA Party. The United States has simply agreed to consider any enterprise owned or controlled by a government as being a state enterprise[11]. Mexico follows this definition but excluded one company, Compania Nacional de Subsistencias Populares, from coverage. Canada has defined the term to cover a Crown corporation under its federal *Financial Administration Act*, or a Crown corporation under comparable provincial law, or any equivalent entity under any applicable provincial law[12].

3. WORKING GROUP

The Parties have agreed to establish a "Trade and Competition" Working Group which will report within five years[13]. This group will report on relevant issues concerning the relationship between competition laws, competition policies and trade in the free trade area. This working group will carry out some of the tasks originally ascribed to another working group under the Canada-U.S. Free Trade Agreement. That agreement provided that the two parties would consult on the use of competition law as a means of harmonizing their differing anti-dumping and countervailing duties law[14]. No agreement on this issue was ever arrived at under the Canada-U.S. Free Trade Agreement.

---

10 NAFTA article 1503(2). An example of such an authority might be the granting of a license.
11 NAFTA article 1505.
12 NAFTA annex 1505. This is a confusing definition which does not seem to be clarified by the *Statement of Government Action* which states at 182 that "corporations with mixed government and private ownership is not covered (*sic*)".
13 NAFTA article 1504.
14 Canada-U.S. Free Trade Agreement article 1906.

16
Temporary Entry for Business Persons

The NAFTA builds upon the framework of the Canada-U.S. Free Trade Agreement which facilitated the cross-border exchange of business persons on a temporary basis. The NAFTA attempts to facilitate temporary entry, not permanent entry. Thus, these provisions do not create a free market in labour between the NAFTA Parties. Instead, the NAFTA establishes temporary entry on a reciprocal basis for business persons.

1. BUSINESS PERSONS

Business persons are defined to be citizens of a NAFTA Party who are engaged in trade in goods, services or investment[1]. Annex 1603 clarifies the categories of business persons. They are:

- business visitors engaged in international activities for the purpose of[2]:

  — research and design;
  — growth, manufacture and production;
  — marketing;
  — sales;
  — distribution;
  — after-sales service; and
  — general service.

- traders who carry on substantial trade in goods or services between their own country and the country they wish to enter[3];

- investors who seek to commit a substantial amount of capital in that country, provided that such persons are employed or operate in a capacity that is supervisory, executive or one that involves essential skills[4];

---

1 NAFTA article 1608.
2 NAFTA appendix 1603.A.1 sets out these provisions clearly.
3 NAFTA annex 1603, Section B, 1.
4 NAFTA annex 1603, Section B, 1(b).

- intra-company transferees employed by a company in a capacity that is managerial or executive or that involves specialized knowledge. To qualify, the transferee must be transferred within the same company to another NAFTA country and must have worked for the company for at least one year within the last three; and

- specified categories of professionals (including lawyers, architects, economists and accountants[5]) meeting the minimum professional requirements set out in the Agreement to engage in business activities at a professional level.

Article 1603 provides that Parties may deny entry to business persons who do not qualify for entry due to public health and safety or national security measures[6]. National authorities may deny temporary entry for the purposes of labour peace[7].

Appendix 1603.D.4 contains special provisions regarding the United States and Mexico. The United States has established an annual limit of 5,500 Mexican professionals entering the U.S. for the first 10 years of the NAFTA's operation. It should be noted that this limit is supplemental to those professionals admitted under a similar category in U.S. domestic law[8] that is capped at 65,000 professionals globally. The United States has reserved the right to increase this limit within the first 10 years of operation[9]. There is no similar agreement between Canada and Mexico.

2. PROVISION OF INFORMATION

Each Party is obliged to provide explanatory material on procedures that business persons may follow to take advantage of the NAFTA temporary entry provisions[10]. Mexico has a one-year deferral from the obligation of providing this information[11].

---

5   The full list is set out in Appendix 1603.D.1 of the NAFTA which is set out at the end of this chapter.

6   NAFTA article 1603(1).

7   Article 1603(2) allows national authorities to bar a person who "might affect adversely": (a) the settlement of a labour dispute that is in progress at the place of employment; or (b) the employment of any person who is involved in such dispute.

8   §101(a)(15)(H)(i)(b) of the *Immigration and Nationality Act*, 1952.

9   NAFTA Appendix 1603.D.4(3).

10   NAFTA article 1604.

11   NAFTA annex 1604.2.

3. NON-COMPLIANCE

A special rule applies to disputes regarding the refusal to grant temporary entry under this NAFTA chapter. No dispute may be pursued under the NAFTA dispute procedures unless two conditions are met:

(a) the matter involves a pattern of practice; and
(b) the business person has exhausted available administrative remedies regarding the matter.

For the purposes of this section, exhaustion of local administrative remedies requires that either a final decision take place, or that the local administrative process take more than one year from the commencement of the action without having an answer[12]. Actions taken by the business person to delay the hearing will not count towards the time limits.

4. CONSULTATIONS

NAFTA article 1605 provides that the Parties will create a Temporary Entry Working Group to consider the operation of this chapter. In addition, the group has a special mandate to review the waiving of labour certification tests to facilitate the entry of spouses of persons who have been granted temporary entry for more than a one-year period[13].

5. PROFESSIONALS WHO QUALIFY FOR TREATMENT UNDER NAFTA CHAPTER 16[14]

(a) GENERAL

Accountant
Architect
Computer Systems Analyst
Disaster Relief Insurance Claims Adjuster
   (claims adjuster employed by an insurance company located in
   the territory of a Party, or an independent claims adjuster)
Economist
Engineer
Forester
Graphic Designer

---

12 NAFTA article 1606(2).
13 NAFTA article 1605(2)(d).
14 A business person seeking temporary entry under this appendix may also perform training functions relating to the profession, including conducting seminars.

Hotel Manager
Industrial Designer
Interior Designer
Land Surveyor
Landscape Architect
Lawyer (including Notary in the Province of Quebec)
Librarian
Management Consultant
Mathematician (including Statistician)
Range Manager/Range Conservationalist
Research Assistant (working in a post-secondary educational
    institution)
Scientific Technician/Technologist[15]
Social Worker
Sylviculturist (including Forestry Specialist)
Technical Publications Writer
Urban Planner (including Geographer)
Vocational Counsellor

(b) MEDICAL/ALLIED PROFESSIONAL

Dentist
Dietician
Medical Laboratory Technologist (Canada)/Medical Technologist
    (Mexico and the United States)[16]
Nutritionist
Occupational Therapist
Pharmacist
Physician (teaching or research only)
Physiotherapist/Physical Therapist
Psychologist
Recreational Therapist
Registered Nurse
Veterinarian

---

15 A business person in this category must be seeking temporary entry to work in direct
    support of professionals in agricultural sciences, astronomy, biology, chemistry, engi-
    neering, forestry, geology, geophysics, meteorology or physics.
16 A business person in this category must be seeking temporary entry to perform in a
    laboratory, chemical, biological, hematological, immunologic, microscopic or bacterio-
    logical tests and analyses for diagnosis, treatment or prevention of disease.

(c) SCIENTIST

Agriculturist (including Agronomist)
Animal Breeder
Animal Scientist
Apiculturist
Astronomer
Biochemist
Biologist
Chemist
Dairy Scientist
Entomologist
Epidemiologist
Geneticist
Geologist
Geochemist
Geophysicist (including Oceanographer in Mexico and the United States)
Horticulturist
Meteorologist
Pharmacologist
Physicist (including Oceanographer in Canada)
Plant Breeder
Poultry Scientist
Soil Scientist
Zoologist

(d) TEACHER

College
Seminary
University

17

Intellectual Property

Intellectual property refers to types of intangible property such as patents, trademarks and copyright which generally grants its holder an exclusive power. This is the exclusive right to use the patent or process within that territory. It also gives the holder the right to take legal action in the case of infringement.

The NAFTA provides protection for intellectual property and an enforcement mechanism to protect these rights. As such, it is the first agreement of its kind to be included within an international trading agreement. Since the Canada-U.S. Free Trade Agreement did not contain a chapter on intellectual property, the NAFTA has built its commitments upon the base of existing international intellectual property treaties and the then-ongoing Uruguay Round negotiations for an agreement on trade-related aspects of intellectual property rights (known as TRIPs).

However, the NAFTA Parties found themselves in different places at the commencement of negotiations. While Canada and the United States were both signatories to major international treaties on intellectual property, and have relatively similar intellectual property systems, Mexico had a very different regime and set of international commitments. Mexico did not have a sophisticated domestic legal regime to deal with copyright and patent infringement. Also, Mexico was not a party to the *Berne Convention*, which sets out key obligations regarding copyright. Given the widespread differences in the treatment of intellectual property rights among the three NAFTA Parties, the NAFTA Intellectual Property chapter provides a comprehensive code of government commitments.

NAFTA establishes minimum standards for the treatment of intellectual property in each of the NAFTA Parties and attempts to prevent intellectual property law from becoming the basis for trade-restrictive actions. The NAFTA obligations set a floor for government conduct. Parties are always able to enact greater protections for intellectual property rights as long as that protection is consistent with the NAFTA[1].

---

1 NAFTA article 1702.

1. EXISTING OBLIGATIONS

The Intellectual Property chapter is based upon the four fundamental international agreements on intellectual property. The NAFTA provides that its Parties must follow their own intellectual property obligations as well as the substantive obligations of four international conventions[2]:

(a) the *Geneva Convention for the Protection of Producers of Phonograms Against Unauthorized Duplication of their Phonograms*, 1971 (Geneva Convention);

(b) the *Berne Convention for the Protection of Literary and Artistic Works*, 1971 (Berne Convention);

(c) the *Paris Convention for the Protection of Industrial Property*, 1967 (Paris Convention); and

(d) the *International Convention for the Protection of New Varieties of Plants*, 1978 (UPOV Convention), or the *International Convention for the Protection of New Varieties of Plants*, 1991 (UPOV Convention).

NAFTA Parties do not have to be members of these conventions, but the failure to meet their substantive provisions would constitute a breach of NAFTA article 1701(2).

2. NAFTA PRINCIPLES

As in other chapters, the NAFTA establishes a set of general principles which are to be the foundation for the Intellectual Property chapter.

(a) NATIONAL TREATMENT

The NAFTA provides that its Parties will provide national treatment in the observation and protection of intellectual property rights. For the Intellectual Property chapter, national treatment applies to the full scope of intellectual property.

One of the difficulties inherent in negotiating an agreement on intellectual property was in the different rights performers hold in the secondary use of their material in Mexico and the United States. In the United States, the copyright holder has all rights on the secondary use of performances while in Mexico it is the performer who retains the rights on secondary use. As a result of these differences, the national treatment obligation includes a provision which applies only to producers or performers of sound recordings on primary use[3].

---

2 NAFTA article 1701(2).
3 NAFTA article 1703(1). This distinction is on account of differences in the treatment of secondary users under Mexican law and American and Canadian law.

National treatment does not apply in cases where judicial or administrative proceedings have been brought for the enforcement of intellectual property rights. This exemption is constrained by the requirement that any judicial measures[4]:

(a) must be necessary to secure compliance with measures that are not inconsistent with the chapter; and
(b) are not applied in a manner that would constitute a disguised restriction on trade.

As well, nothing in the NAFTA will prevent a Party from creating laws to prevent the infringement of intellectual property as an anti-competitive practice[5].

The national treatment obligation applies not only to the recognition of rights, but also to their enforcement[6]. There are provisions of intellectual property enforcement legislation which treat foreign rights differently from domestic ones. In 1983, a GATT panel reviewing this topic[7] ruled that this provision of American law violated the GATT national treatment obligation[8]. The NAFTA specifically requires its Parties to abide by the national treatment obligation. However, while the NAFTA required this change, the American NAFTA implementation legislation did not include any change to this section[9].

(b) COPYRIGHT

The NAFTA contains provisions regarding extending protection to copyright holders. A key issue in the minds of NAFTA negotiators was the treatment of new kinds of intellectual property which had not been enumerated in the Berne Convention, such as software or encrypted satellite transmissions. The NAFTA has provided for very broad copyright protection. Article 1705(1) sets out a significant modification to those works protected by article 2 of the Berne Convention. The NAFTA states:

> Each Party shall protect the works covered by Article 2 of the Berne Convention, including any other works that embody original expression within the meaning of that Convention. In particular:

---

4 NAFTA article 1703(3).
5 NAFTA article 1704.
6 NAFTA article 1703(1).
7 That is, s. 337 of the *Tariff Act*.
8 Report of the Panel, United States - Imports of Certain Automotive Spring Assemblies, adopted May 26, 1983. GATT, BISD, 30 Supp. 107 (1984).
9 The Canadians have made a note of this in their *Statement of Government Action* at 196.

(a) all types of computer programs are literary works within the meaning of the Berne Convention and each Party shall protect them as such; and

(b) compilations of data or other material, whether in machine-readable or other form, which by reason of the selection or arrangement of their contents constitute intellectual creations, shall be protected as such.

The inclusion of the term "other works that embody original expression" in paragraph one leads to the clear application of the chapter's obligations to the widest possible interpretation of intellectual property.

The NAFTA also prevents the rental of computer software where the essential object of the rental is duplication[10]. Since Canadian law did not contain this prohibition, this commitment required a change in Canadian practices on January 1, 1994[11].

The NAFTA includes provisions on sound recordings which give producers greater rights over reproduction, importation, distribution and rentals. The NAFTA provides copyright protection for sound recordings for at least 50 years[12].

(c) PATENTS

The NAFTA contains comprehensive provisions on the protection of patents within the North American market. The NAFTA provides that its Parties must make patents available for all inventions that "are new, result from an inventive step and are capable of industrial application"[13]. This includes items such as microorganisms and non-biological plant or animal production[14].

The NAFTA provides that Parties may provide exceptions to patent rights[15]:

provided that such exceptions do not unreasonably conflict with a normal exploitation of the patent and do not unreasonably prejudice the legitimate interests of the patent owner, taking into account the legitimate interests of other persons.

The meaning of this clause is somewhat ambiguous. Some American legal commentators have suggested that the interpretation of this clause

---

10 NAFTA article 1705(2).
11 Section 55(2) of the Canadian *NAFTA Implementation Act* changed the Canadian *Copyright Act* to put an end to these practices on the NAFTA's implementation.
12 NAFTA article 1706(2).
13 NAFTA article 1709(1).
14 NAFTA article 1709(3).
15 NAFTA article 1709(6).

will make a difference on the effectiveness of the NAFTA patent protections[16].

Patent protection will run for a period of 20 years from the date of filing or 17 years from the date of the grant of the patent[17]. Parties may extend the term of the patent protection to compensate for delays caused by the regulatory approval process.

The NAFTA sets out a general prohibition on compulsory licensing except in cases where "such exceptions do not unreasonably conflict with a normal exploitation of the patent and do not unreasonably prejudice the legitimate interests of the patent owner, taking into account the legitimate interests of other persons"[18]. These obligations go further than those contained in the Uruguay Round TRIPs agreement.

It should be noted that the NAFTA does not deal with the issue of parallel imports[19]. Parallel imports, also known as "grey marketing", occur when a good is legally produced under rights in one jurisdiction and imported into the market of another country where the product rights are held by someone else. Thus, there is a conflict between two products which are both legally produced in the home jurisdiction. This has been a very difficult question to resolve in common markets such as the European Union, for it establishes a conflict between the free movement of goods and the territoriality inherent in intellectual property law[20].

Chapter 21 of the NAFTA also provides an exemption from the Agreement for measures with respect to Canadian cultural industries[21].

---

16 See Charles Levy and Stuart Walker "The NAFTA: A Watershed for Protection of Intellectual Property Law", 27 *The International Lawyer* 671 at 681. They wrote:
> The double use of "unreasonably" - a vague standard- and the reference to the interests of third parties allow broad interpretation of this language. If signatories to the NAFTA do adopt a broad interpretation of this language, much of the protection given to patent holders could effectively be negated.

17 NAFTA article 1709(12).

18 NAFTA article 1709(6). It should be noted that finding these conditions would be very difficult indeed. The NAFTA essentially prevents compulsory licensing regimes from returning in Canada and Mexico.

19 *Statement of Administrative Action* at 189.

20 The two key European Union cases on parallel imports give an excellent understanding to the complexities of these issues. They are *Deutsche Grammaphon v. Metro*, [1971] E.C.R. 487; [1971] C.M.L.R. 631 and *Centrafarm v. Sterling Drug*, [1974] E.C.R. 1147; [1974] 2 C.M.L.R. 480.

21 This exemption does not exclude the tariff-related measures contained in article 302. The cultural industries exemption is examined in some detail in chapter 25 of this book.

(d) OTHER INTELLECTUAL PROPERTY RIGHTS

The NAFTA deals with intellectual property beyond copyright and patents. NAFTA Parties have committed to keep secret any trade secrets disclosed by businesses for the purposes of safety and effectiveness under government requirement[22]. The NAFTA contains provisions which give protection to other types of intellectual property rights and the public such as:

- for integrated circuits[23], these rights extend to the circuits themselves and the articles which incorporate them[24];

- the prevention of the misleading use of geographical indications for products and trademarks. Geographical indications which are used in good faith may continue[25];

- new and original industrial designs. NAFTA Parties undertake to make requirements for securing protection of textile designs easier to comply with and more cost effective[26]; and

- trademarks, including service marks. These protections are both substantive and procedural. Article 1708(4) lays out specific minimum registration procedures with which NAFTA Parties must comply.

The NAFTA requires its Parties to amend their criminal laws to ban the sale of devices which allow the public to improperly access encrypted satellite signals[27]. Parties must also amend their civil law to make it an offence to improperly receive and decode these signals[28].

(e) ENFORCEMENT PROCEDURES

An important consideration for NAFTA negotiators was to establish a system for the enforcement of intellectual property rights in Mexico, which did not have a comprehensive enforcement mechanism for intellectual property. Thus, the NAFTA requires its parties to amend their domestic

---

22 NAFTA article 1711.
23 NAFTA article 1710(2).
24 NAFTA article 1710(c).
25 NAFTA article 1712(4). Thus presumably companies such as Canada Dry will be able to use their trade names without fear of this NAFTA provision, but a product such as Mexican produced water called "Yukon Water" might conflict with this rule.
26 NAFTA article 1713(2).
27 NAFTA article 1707(a).
28 NAFTA article 1707(b).

laws to include specific enforcement obligations which must be fair and not unnecessarily complicated[29].

The NAFTA requires provisions in the civil and criminal laws of each party dealing with intellectual property crimes such as counterfeiting. Also, domestic measures must provide for a degree of transparency such as requiring that decisions of tribunals adjudicating intellectual property rights be in writing and be based on the evidence before the tribunals. Parties must provide for judicial review of these decisions[30].

Parties may create a separate judicial process for enforcing intellectual property rights, but this is not required by the NAFTA[31]. Legal protections are laid out in article 1715(1). These include the following:

(a) defendants have the right to written notice that is timely and contains sufficient detail, including the basis of the claims;
(b) parties in a proceeding are allowed to be represented by independent legal counsel;
(c) the procedures do not include the imposition of overly burdensome requirements concerning mandatory personal appearances;
(d) all parties in a proceeding are duly entitled to substantiate their claims and to present relevant evidence; and
(e) the procedures include a means to identify and protect confidential information.

In addition, the NAFTA requires that courts have the authority to order injunctive relief. This was an entirely new addition to the civil law in Mexico and an important consideration for the American NAFTA negotiators.

The NAFTA requires that border enforcement take place to detain copyright-protected goods[32]. Border enforcement measures took place on January 1, 1994 between Canada and the United States. Border measures are not scheduled to begin until 1997 between Mexico and the United States.

---

29 NAFTA article 1714(2).
30 NAFTA article 1714(4).
31 NAFTA article 1714(5) specifically makes this clear.
32 NAFTA article 1718.

18

Publication, Notification and Administration of Laws

Numerous provisions in the NAFTA provide investment and trade opportunities for private individuals and businesses[1]. With these opportunities comes a commensurate need to know of those government actions that affect areas covered by the NAFTA. The GATT was the first trade agreement to require the publication of government measures, but it only imposed these obligations on trade regulations[2]. The NAFTA expands these obligations much further by requiring the publication and review of "measures of general application" affecting matters covered by the Agreement[3]. It also provides an opportunity, where practible, for NAFTA citizens to raise concerns over changes which could affect their rights under the NAFTA[4]. NAFTA governments are also provided with an opportunity to comment on these proposed laws to the maximum extent possible[5].

1. PUBLICATION

An important development in the NAFTA is that it requires its Parties to make information available to the public. The NAFTA imposes a publication requirement on all laws, regulations, procedures and administrative rulings of general application[6]. This is an absolute obligation upon the NAFTA Parties. In addition, the Agreement establishes a number of transparency obligations which should provide minimum guarantees of procedural due process. Thus, this NAFTA chapter attempts to provide dispute

---

1 Such publication and notification requirements arise in the Government Procurement, Cross-Border Services and Telecommunications chapters and the notification requirement regarding the modification of domestic antidumping and countervailing laws in chapter 19.
2 GATT Article X.
3 NAFTA article 1806 defines this to mean government actions which apply to all and affect a matter covered by the Agreement, not including judicial or judicial-like rulings.
4 NAFTA article 1802(2).
5 NAFTA article 1802(2).
6 NAFTA article 1802(1). This provision is similar to article 2102 of the Canada-U.S. Free Trade Agreement.

settlement and the making of laws and regulations in an open, accessible and fair manner.

2. NOTIFICATION

A Party is required to inform the other Parties whenever it proposes a measure which could materially affect the operation of the NAFTA or a Party's interest under it[7]. For example, this obligation would require a NAFTA Party to notify the other Parties if it was contemplating a change to its domestic product standards. While Parties may make changes to their domestic laws as they see fit, they must notify the other Parties in advance. Parties must also answer questions posed by other Parties on the proposed measure. In order to foster communication between the Parties, each NAFTA government must designate a contact point to facilitate communications on any matter covered by the NAFTA[8].

3. ADMINISTRATIVE PROCEEDINGS AND REVIEW

Persons who are directly affected by measures which affect the operation of the NAFTA must have certain procedural rights. These rights include having reasonable notice of a proceeding, including knowledge of the issues in dispute, the right to attend the hearing and to participate in it, and a right to independent judicial review[9]. These obligations mirror existing GATT obligations[10].

Parties are required to put in place judicial or quasi-judicial procedures to review administrative actions covered by the NAFTA. The NAFTA guarantees that these tribunals must be impartial, independent and not have any interest in the outcome of the matter[11]. In addition, litigants are granted procedural rights such as the right to support their positions, and to have a decision which is based on the evidence and submissions before the tribunal[12].

---

7 NAFTA article 1803(1).
8 NAFTA article 1801.
9 NAFTA article 1804(a).
10 GATT Articles X:1 and X:3.
11 NAFTA article 1805.
12 NAFTA article 1805(2).

4. NAFTA DISPUTE-SETTLEMENT PROCESS

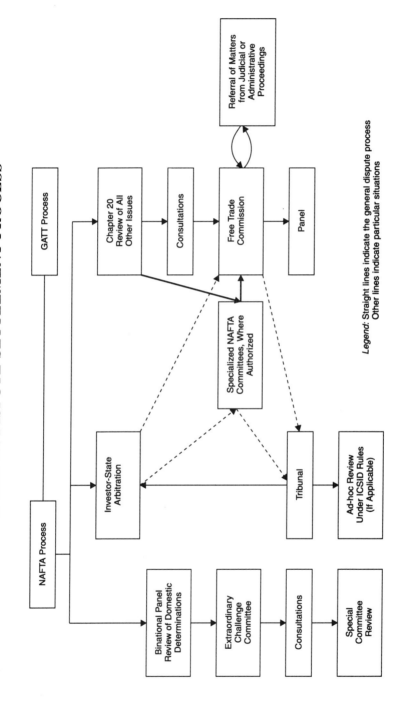

Legend: Straight lines indicate the general dispute process
Other lines indicate particular situations

19

Antidumping and Countervailing Duty Matters

In the 1980's, the trading relationship between Canada and the United States was marked by a number of trade-related disputes over such matters as steel, lumber, pork and fish. Many of these disputes were based on the thorny issue of what government practices constituted a subsidy to business. A principal goal behind the Canadian and American decision to enter into the Canada-U.S. Free Trade Agreement was to reduce the uncertainty in bilateral trade relations caused by the intensity of those disputes regarding subsidies and antidumping. Negotiations on this bilateral agreement almost failed over the sensitive issue of defining a common understanding on subsidies. As a compromise solution, the Canada-U.S. Free Trade Agreement established an innovative system to review the final countervailing or antidumping duty decisions in each Party. The agreement established that domestic courts would no longer have the right to provide final review for domestic countervailing and antidumping duty determinations. Instead, the Canada-U.S. Free Trade Agreement provided that the final review of the decisions of domestic agencies would occur through a special binational panel[1]. These panels would apply the domestic law where the dispute took place, including its domestic standard of judicial review[2]. Panels would be required to make their decisions on a very strict timetable[3] which was to compare favourably with the time required for full judicial review.

This binational review process was conceived of as a temporary measure under the agreement. The provisions were only to be in force for a total of seven years or until such time as the Parties developed a substitute system of rules for subsidies and antidumping duties[4]. However, by the entry into

---

1 Canada-U.S. Free Trade Agreement article 1904(1).
2 Canada-U.S. Free Trade Agreement articles 1904(3) and 1911.
3 Canada-U.S. Free Trade Agreement article 1904(14) sets out a timetable which requires review within 315 days from the date of an initial request for review.
4 Canada-U.S. Free Trade Agreement article 1906.

force of the NAFTA, five years later, no substitute system of rules for subsidies and antidumping was reached.

The NAFTA carried forward the basic process for the settlement of subsidies and antidumping questions from the Canada-U.S. Free Trade Agreement with several relatively minor modifications. However, unlike the earlier agreement, the NAFTA does not provide for any sunset period for its binational panel provisions, nor does it obligate its Parties to achieve any harmonization in their domestic subsidies and antidumping laws. The NAFTA permits each Party to retain its own antidumping and countervailing duty laws[5] and to use them[6], subject to certain minimum standards[7]. However, the NAFTA imposes some procedural limits on these changes. Parties who wish to modify their own trade laws must first abide by the specific notification rules set out in article 1902(2)(b) and the more general notification obligations in NAFTA chapter 18[8]. If another NAFTA Party believes that a modification to another Party's trade remedy laws would be inconsistent with the NAFTA, a panel can be formed to review the proposed legislation[9].

1. BINATIONAL DISPUTE SETTLEMENT PANELS

The NAFTA substitutes domestic judicial review of domestic antidumping and countervailing duty decisions with binational panel review[10]. Thus NAFTA Parties agree that for questions on the review of antidumping and countervailing duty proceedings, their own court systems will not be the final arbiter. Instead, NAFTA binational panels will provide final review of domestic administrative determinations based on the same domestic antidumping and countervailing duty laws of the importing Party. The NAFTA provides that antidumping or countervailing duty laws consist of the relevant statutes, legislative history, regulations, administrative practices and judicial precedents to the extent that a court of the importing Party would rely on such materials in reviewing a final determination of the competent investigating authority[11].

Binational panels to review final antidumping and countervailing duty determinations may be commenced by a NAFTA Party on its own, or on

---

5 NAFTA article 1902(1).
6 For example, §102(a)(2)(b) of the U.S. implementing legislation maintains this right.
7 NAFTA annex 1904.15 sets out required changes to each Party's trade laws. Most of the substantive changes apply to Mexico which agreed to bring its trade law regime closer to the Canadian and American models.
8 NAFTA article 1803(1).
9 NAFTA article 1903(1).
10 NAFTA article 1904(1).
11 NAFTA article 1904(2).

the request of a person who would otherwise be entitled under domestic law to commence judicial review[12]. Persons who have a right to commence a binational panel also have the right to be represented at its hearings[13].

(a) COMPOSITION OF PANELS

NAFTA panels are comprised of five members who are chosen from rosters which have been submitted by the Parties. Roster members must be of good character, have sound judgment and be familiar with international trade law[14]. The NAFTA states that, to the extent practicable, Parties are to name judges or former judges to the roster[15]. Each disputing Party may name two panellists from the roster. If a Party wishes to select a panellist whose name does not appear on the roster, the other disputing Party has a right to automatically disqualify up to four of these non-roster candidates[16]. A fifth panellist will be selected by consensus between the Parties[17]. Once all the panellists are selected, they will decide among themselves on a chair, who must be a lawyer[18].

(b) PANEL DECISION-MAKING

NAFTA binational panels conduct their review on the basis of the domestic trade laws of the importing Party. The NAFTA does not create a common set of trade laws for the free trade area. Each Party's trade laws are incorporated into the NAFTA for the purposes of panel review[19]. The panels are asked merely to apply the appropriate standard of review of the Party. When making these decisions, panels must apply the general legal principles that would be applied by a court in the importing Party[20]. Annex 1911 sets out a different standard of review in each of the NAFTA Parties. The standards are as follows:

---

12 NAFTA article 1904(5).
13 NAFTA article 1904(7).
14 NAFTA annex 1901.2(1).
15 NAFTA annex 1901.2(1). Canada has noted in its *Statement of Government Action* (at 204) that it intends to nominate persons who are learned in international law who are not judges.
16 NAFTA annex 1901.2(2).
17 NAFTA annex 1901.2(3). If consensus cannot be found, the annex details a procedure on how a fifth panellist will be selected by lot.
18 NAFTA annex 1901.2(4).
19 NAFTA article 1904(2). Thus, to this extent, domestic laws have become part of the international agreement.
20 NAFTA article 1904(2).

(a) in the case of Canada, the agency failed to observe a principle of natural justice, erred in law when making its decision or based its decision on an erroneous finding of fact[21];

(b) in the case of the United States, that the agency decision is unsupported by substantial evidence on the record or unsupported otherwise by rule of law; and

(c) in the case of Mexico, the standard set forth in Article 238 of the *Código Fiscal de la Federación*, or any successor statutes, based solely on the administrative record[22].

The standard of review in Canada differs from the United States as Canadian courts allow greater discretion to administrating agencies[23]. This results in making binational panel review more difficult to obtain in Canada than in the United States. This difference in the standard of review may account for part of the asymmetry in seeking binational panel review under the Canada-U.S. Free Trade Agreement. For example, Washington trade counsel Homer Moyer, Jr. points out that of the 31 binational panel reviews taken under the agreement, 23 have been reviews of American agency determinations[24]. An additional reason that may account for this trend is the differences in litigation attitudes between Canada and the United States. While Americans have tended to view trade remedy laws as "merely another arrow in the quiver of American business", Canadians tend to rely on litigious solutions to a much lesser degree in the normal course[25].

(c) TIMING

The NAFTA has reproduced the identical terms of the Canada-U.S. Free Trade Agreement regarding the timing for panel decisions[26]. The NAFTA requires each Party to produce detailed rules of procedure for the

---

21 These are the grounds set forth in s. 18.1(4) of the *Federal Court Act* with respect to all final determinations.

22 In NAFTA annex 1904.14, Schedule of Mexico (u), Mexico commits to amend its laws to provide that this standard of review apply to binational panels.

23 The Supreme Court of Canada has established that the standard of review must be based on the tribunal making a decision that was "patently unreasonable". This was recently considered by the court in *National Corn Growers Assn. v. Canada (Canadian Import Tribunal)*, [1990] 2 S.C.R. 1324. This standard was maintained again in *Domtar Inc. v. Québec (Commission d'appel en matière de lésions professionnelles)*, [1993] 2 S.C.R. 756 (indexed as *Domtar v. Québec*). Canadian courts are much less likely to review administrative decisions than comparable American courts.

24 Homer Moyer, Jr. "Chapter 19 of the NAFTA: Binational Panels as the Trade Courts of Last Resort", 27 *The International Lawyer* 707 at 709-710.

25 The author is indebted to Barry Campbell, noted Canadian trade counsel and Member of Parliament, for his helpful observations on this and other points.

26 Canada-U.S. Free Trade Agreement article 1904(14).

handling of antidumping and countervailing duty disputes before panels[27]. NAFTA article 1904(14) requires that the Parties prepare rules of procedure. This article continues to state that:

> The rules shall be designed to result in final decisions within 315 days of the date on which a request for a panel is made, and shall allow:
>
> (a) 30 days for the filing of the complaint;
> (b) 30 days for designation or certification of the administrative record and its filing with the panel;
> (c) 60 days for the complainant to file its brief;
> (d) 60 days for the respondent to file its brief;
> (e) 15 days for the filing of reply briefs;
> (f) 15 to 30 days for the panel to convene and hear oral argument; and
> (g) 90 days for the panel to issue its written decision.

Panel decisions may only be brought within 60 days of the publication of the final determination of an antidumping or countervailing duty[28]. Panels may also be established on the imposition of provisional measures in an inves igation[29]. The NAFTA provides that Parties may not allow their domestic legislation to provide for appeals of questions on their domestic laws which have been decided by panels[30]. Thus, to this extent, the decisions of the binational panels are final and binding.

2. PANEL REVIEW OF LEGISLATIVE CHANGES

In addition to permitting binational review of the final domestic antidumping and countervailing decisions, the NAFTA allows for dispute panel review where a Party alleges that another Party's proposed antidumping or countervailing duty measure is inconsistent with the obligations in the Agreement or the GATT[31]. If a panel determines that the proposed legislation is inconsistent with the NAFTA or the GATT, the Parties must consult to resolve the dispute[32]. Should consultations fail, the Party requesting the review may take comparable legislative or administrative action or terminate the Agreement on 60 days written notice[33].

---

27 Rules of procedure to govern the panel process were published by Canada and the United States at *Canada Gazette*, Jan. 12, 1994 and 59 F.R. 229.
28 NAFTA article 1904(4).
29 NAFTA article 1904(4).
30 NAFTA article 1904(11).
31 NAFTA article 1903(1). Article 1906(b) makes clear that this only applies to amendments enacted after Jan. 1, 1994.
32 NAFTA article 1903(3).
33 NAFTA article 1903(3)(b).

3. EXTRAORDINARY CHALLENGE COMMITTEES

The NAFTA, like the Canada-U.S. Free Trade Agreement, permits the review of the decision of a binational panel where the integrity of the panel comes into question. The Extraordinary Challenge Committee (EEC) may review panel decisions if:

- there is an allegation of gross misconduct[34] on the panel;

- the panel seriously departed from a fundamental rule of procedure[35]; or

- the panel manifestly exceeded its powers, authority or jurisdiction such as failing to apply the appropriate standard of review[36].

In order to bring an Extraordinary Challenge, it is necessary to allege one of these grounds and that there has also been an alleged material affect to the improper action which threatens the integrity of the binational panel process[37]. This process is only available to NAFTA Parties. Individual litigants who may be involved in the panel review do not have a right to seek an Extraordinary Challenge. Committees of three panellists will be struck within 15 days of a request by a Party[38]. Once established, the committee has 90 days to reach a decision[39].

Extraordinary Challenges are not designed to act as an appeal court for disputants who are displeased with the results of the panels. Rather, the panels are designed to consider issues of impropriety which bring the entire system of panel review into question. After hearing a challenge, an Extraordinary Challenge Committee may dismiss the challenge, vacate the original panel proceeding and/or constitute a new panel[40].

Professor Andreas Lowenfeld has suggested that there is some risk in having an Extraordinary Challenge process contained in the NAFTA (and the earlier bilateral agreement). He suggested that since the Extraordinary Challenge Committee is comprised primarily of former judges, and not trade experts, the committees could act more like an appeal court than a

---

34 This includes such matters as bias, a serious conflict of interest or other material violations of the rules of conduct: NAFTA article 1904(13)(a)(i).

35 NAFTA article 1904(13)(a)(ii).

36 NAFTA article 1904(13)(a)(iii).

37 NAFTA article 1904(13)(b).

38 NAFTA annex 1904.13(1).

39 NAFTA annex 1904.13(2).

40 NAFTA article 1904(8).

review body[41]. While the use of Extraordinary Challenge Committees under the Canada-U.S. Free Trade Agreement did not use the committees like courts of appeal, there were too few cases to be able to fundamentally establish a trend[42]. Accordingly, under the NAFTA, this risk continues.

(a) THE EXTRAORDINARY CHALLENGES UNDER THE CANADA-U.S. FREE TRADE AGREEMENT AND THE NAFTA

Within the NAFTA, its Parties attempted to clarify a lingering dispute between Canada and the United States over the grounds on which an Extraordinary Challenge could be based. Unfortunately, the attempt to clarify the issue has itself lead to disagreement. The basis for this disagreement arises from decisions of dispute panels under the Canada-U.S. Free Trade Agreement which centred on the question of how to apply domestic trade law[43]. Specifically, the dispute centres on the meaning of NAFTA article 1904(13)(a)(iii) which allows Extraordinary Challenge Committee review if:

> the panel manifestly exceeded its powers, authority or jurisdiction set out in this article, for example by failing to apply the appropriate standard of review.

The American *Statement of Administrative Action* interprets the NAFTA to allow a broader basis for court review of the binding binational panel decisions than allowed under the Canada-U.S. Free Trade Agreement[44]. The *Statement of Administrative Action* states that[45]:

> Any failure by a binational panel to apply the appropriate standard of review, if such failure materially affected the outcome of the panel process and threatened the integrity of the binational panel review process, would be grounds for an ECC to vacate or remand a panel decision.

---

41 These comments are taken in the light of the arbitral practice under ICSID which had its process of ad-hoc review of arbitral awards used as an appeal vehicle by unsatisfied litigants. A. Lowenfeld "The Free Trade Agreement Meets its First Challenge: Dispute Settlement and the Pork Case", (1992) 37 *McGill L.J.* 597 at 620.

42 There were only two Extraordinary Challenges raised under the Canada-U.S. Free Trade Agreement and neither of these challenges successfully overturned a panel decision.

43 The case at the heart of this controversy is the panel decision on Fresh, Chilled or Frozen Pork from Canada (USA-89-1904-11). The U.S. government attempted to have this decision reviewed by an Extraordinary Challenge Committee on the basis that American trade law was misapplied. The panel rejected the request for the Extraordinary Challenge.

44 *Statement of Administrative Action* at 195.

45 *Statement of Administrative Action* at 196.

The decisions of a few binational panels convened under the CFTA have underscored the importance of the NAFTA's emphasis on the proper application of the judicial standard of review. In specific, these decisions have raised the question of whether these panels have correctly applied the standard of review. Where, in the Administration's view, panel decisions have failed to apply to appropriate standard of review or they have otherwise manifestly exceeded their powers, authority or jurisdiction, there could be recourse to the extraordinary challenge procedure under Article 1904(13).

The American NAFTA implementing legislation provides that Americans can appeal decisions of panels to an Extraordinary Challenge Committee if there is a disagreement with a panel interpretation. This view is not shared by the government of Canada. The *Statement of Government Action* provides the Canadian position on the basis for appeal to Extraordinary Challenge Committees. It states that the wording of the NAFTA does not change the basis for review that was established under the Canada-U.S. Free Trade Agreement[46]. Thus, the Canadian government has recorded its different interpretation on this issue for the record. The *Statement of Government Action* suggests that referral of disputes to national courts is not permitted by the terms of NAFTA article 1905(7).

Rather than solving this contentious issue through the text of the NAFTA, it appears that Canada and the United States have laid the foundation for a future dispute which may have to be settled by a NAFTA dispute panel.

4. SPECIAL COMMITTEES

The NAFTA provides a final body to safeguard the review process. A "special committee", not provided for in the Canada-U.S. Free Trade Agreement, will ensure that the panel process works as intended. A Party may request a special committee to determine if another Party's laws:

- prevent the establishment of a panel;
- prevent a panel from rendering a decision;
- prevent the implementation of a panel decision; or
- fail to provide an opportunity for panel or judicial review.

If a Party makes any of these allegations, it may call for consultations within 15 days[47]. If there is no resolution within 45 days, then a special committee may be formed.

---

46 *Statement of Government Action* at 204.
47 NAFTA article 1905(1).

Special committees are comprised of three members chosen from a special roster[48] comprised of former judges[49]. Committees must come to a decision within 90 days of their establishment[50]. If the special committee makes an affirmative finding, the Parties are to consult with a view to resolving the matter[51]. Should the matter remain unresolved, the complaining Party can suspend the operation of the binational system as it applies to that Party[52] or may retaliate in an appropriate fashion[53].

5. SECRETARIAT

The NAFTA expands upon the temporary secretariat created by the Canada-U.S. Free Trade Agreement by creating a permanent one[54]. This institution acts as a registry for complaints and a coordinating body for the NAFTA's many commissions, committees and working groups[55].

6. WORKING GROUPS

In November, 1993, the governments of the United States and Canada made public an Understanding which sought to reduce disputes concerning subsidies, dumping and the operation of trade-remedy laws[56]. They agreed to create two additional working groups which were not initially created by the NAFTA. These working groups will deal with issues of subsidies and antidumping and will report back to the Free Trade Commission by December 31, 1995.

NAFTA Parties are also obliged to hold annual consultations to consider problems regarding the operation and implementation of the chapter. They have also committed to consult on more effective rules and disciplines regarding the use of government subsidies and transborder pricing.

---

48 NAFTA article 1905(4). This roster is the same from which Extraordinary Challenge Committee members are named.

49 NAFTA annex 1904.13(1).

50 NAFTA annex 1904.13(2).

51 NAFTA article 1905(7).

52 NAFTA article 1905(8)(a).

53 NAFTA article 1905(8)(b). It should be noted that the special committee has the power to review whether the retaliation is appropriate to the circumstances (NAFTA article 1905(10)(a)).

54 NAFTA article 2002.

55 The International Coordinating Secretariat has taken over many of the functions originally designated for the NAFTA secretariat. This Coordinating Secretariat is discussed in chapter 20 of this book.

56 This understanding is referred to in the *Statement of Government Action* at 207.

20

Institutional Arrangements and Dispute Settlement

In addition to the detailed dispute settlement provisions for counter-vailing and antidumping duty issues, the NAFTA creates ongoing institutions to oversee its implementation, operation, interpretation and to settle its disputes. NAFTA Parties who have a dispute may raise an issue either under the GATT dispute settlement process or the NAFTA. Before any dispute can be formally raised against another Party at the GATT on an issue covered by the NAFTA, the complaining Party is obligated to notify the other Party. The NAFTA provides that if the Parties cannot agree amongst themselves, then a dispute shall "normally" be settled under the NAFTA[1].

If a dispute involves factual issues regarding standards-related environmental, safety, health or conservation measures, or if the dispute arises under specific environmental agreements, then the dispute may only be considered under the NAFTA process[2]. The only parties which may appear in these hearings are national governments. Interested parties and local or subnational governments may not appear, even if the dispute centres around their activities[3].

1. THE FREE TRADE COMMISSION

The NAFTA has created the Free Trade Commission (FTC) as the political structure of the Agreement. The FTC is comprised of cabinet-level representatives of each NAFTA Party. It is similar in its structure to the

---

1 NAFTA article 2005. What does the term "normally" mean? A country could certainly suggest that any dispute would constitute an extraordinary situation. This provision is not subject to NAFTA dispute settlement according to note 46 at N-8.

2 NAFTA article 2005(3).

3 It should be noted that the *Statement of Government Action* at 214 states that Canada will consult closely with its provinces in the preparation and presentation of chapter 20 proceedings where provincial measures are at issue. There is no similar guarantee for local governments and no guidance on the American position is provided in the *Statement of Administrative Action*.

GATT Council. The FTC has the authority to supervise all work of NAFTA committees and working groups[4]. A domestic judicial or administrative tribunal may refer any interpretative question in any action to the FTC. It has the power to make interpretive rulings on the NAFTA which will be binding on dispute resolution panels. It does not appear that the interpretations of the Commission will be binding on the domestic courts[5].

2. THE NAFTA SECRETARIAT

The NAFTA creates a Secretariat with national offices in each NAFTA Party. Article 2002(3) provides that the Secretariat shall:

(a) provide assistance to the Free Trade Commission;
(b) provide administrative assistance to chapter 19 and 20 dispute resolution panels; and
(c) support the work of other NAFTA bodies at the direction of the Free Trade Commission and otherwise facilitate the operation of this Agreement.

At the first meeting of the Free Trade Commission, the Parties created an International Coordinating Secretariat for the NAFTA based in Mexico City. Many of the functions of the Free Trade Commission Secretariat have been transferred to this International Coordinating Secretariat[6]. It will assist the Free Trade Commission in facilitating the activities of the NAFTA subcommittees and working groups[7]. The Coordinating Secretariat will have a different role from the NAFTA Secretariat, which will focus on keeping records regarding antidumping and countervailing reviews and NAFTA disputes under chapter 20.

3. INSTITUTIONAL DISPUTE SETTLEMENT

The NAFTA provides for the settlement of disputes by panels. A dispute occurs under the NAFTA where a Party has taken, or is proposing to take, an action that is inconsistent with the Agreement. Also, as in the

---

4 NAFTA article 2001.
5 This makes the FTC interpretation far less useful than the interpretations that a court may seek from the European Court of Justice in similar circumstances under article 177 of the *Treaty of Rome* (1957), 298 U.N.T.S. 11.
6 The International Coordinating Secretariat was given those duties of the Free Trade Secretariat in NAFTA article 2002(3)(c). At the time of writing, NAFTA Parties had been discussing changing the name of this Secretariat to the North American Trade Secretariat. *Inside NAFTA*, April 20, 1994 at 1.
7 *Inside NAFTA*, Jan. 14, 1994 at 1.

GATT[8], a dispute could also be commenced where a Party's action allegedly causes nullification or impairment of benefits which a Party could reasonably expect under the NAFTA[9]. To establish a nullification or impairment complaint, it is necessary to show that the otherwise NAFTA-consistent measure of a Party has resulted in the impairment of an expected NAFTA benefit and the taking of this measure by the Party had not been reasonably foreseen at the time the Agreement was negotiated. Nullification and impairment is available to base a dispute regarding goods[10], intellectual property rights and services. It may not be used to deal with matters such as cross-border services or intellectual property which are covered by the general NAFTA exceptions in article 2101[11].

Before a dispute can be raised by a NAFTA Party to a panel, the Parties must complete a process of consultations. Only after consultations have occurred, may a dispute panel be struck.

(a) THE CONSULTATION PROCESS

A Party may request a meeting of the Free Trade Commission within 30 days to discuss any matter under dispute[12]. The purpose of this meeting is to resolve the dispute and avoid further action. The NAFTA requires that in certain cases, technical bodies replace the Free Trade Commission's consultations. This will occur regarding issues on rules of origin, sanitary and phytosanitary standards and standards-related measures. In addition, the Environmental Supplemental Agreement to the NAFTA stipulates that the Environmental Council may provide assistance to the Free Trade Commission in consultations regarding the failure to observe NAFTA article 1114[13].

(b) PANEL DISPUTE SETTLEMENT

Should the Free Trade Commission be unable to resolve the dispute, then a Party may request it to create a dispute resolution panel. Any other Party who believes that it has a "substantive interest" in the matter is entitled to join the dispute as a complaining Party[14] or as a non-complaining

---

8 GATT Article XXIII.
9 NAFTA article 2004.
10 NAFTA annex 2004(1)(a) excludes goods in automotive trade or energy issues related to investment.
11 NAFTA annex 2004(2).
12 NAFTA article 2008(3).
13 Environmental Supplemental Agreement article 10(6)(b).
14 NAFTA article 2008(3).

Party[15]. Disputes dealing with the environment, safety, health or conservation may be referred to scientific review boards to address factual issues before a dispute panel is struck[16].

A panel of five members may be chosen from a roster comprised of national nominees[17]. Panellists must have expertise in law, international trade, matters covered by the agreement or the resolution of international disputes[18]. In all disputes, the disputing Parties must endeavour to name a chair of the panel within 15 days of its creation[19]. For disputes between two Parties, each Party is required to name two panellists. Each panellist must be a citizen of the other disputing Party[20]. If more than two Parties are involved in the dispute, the defending Party is required to name a panellist from each of the complaining Parties. Then the other disputing Parties may jointly name two panellists who are citizens of the defending Party[21].

The Free Trade Commission may make rules of procedure for panels[22]. The panel must issue its initial report within 90 days of the last panellist being chosen[23]. This initial report will then be sent to the Parties for comment. Wherever possible, the resolution of the dispute will involve the elimination of the measure in dispute. Failing that, the panels may award compensation[24].

(c) PANEL DECISIONS

A final report must be submitted to the Parties 30 days after the initial report is issued[25]. The defending Party must implement this report, offer appropriate compensation or the complaining Party may retaliate by suspending equivalent benefits[26]. A non-complaining Party may not participate in the retaliation.

Any suspension taken as a retaliation for the failure of a NAFTA Party to comply with a report can be reviewed by a panel if it is manifestly

---

15 NAFTA article 2013.
16 NAFTA article 2015.
17 NAFTA article 2011.
18 NAFTA article 2009(2).
19 NAFTA articles 2011(1)(b) and 2011(2)(b).
20 NAFTA article 2011(1)(c).
21 NAFTA article 2011(2)(c). This is a novel means of striking arbitral panels. Other agreements have provisions which allow governments to name their own nationals to panels. No other agreement requires a Party to name the national of the disputing Party to the panel.
22 NAFTA article 2012.
23 NAFTA article 2016.
24 NAFTA article 2018(2).
25 NAFTA article 2017(1).
26 NAFTA article 2009.

excessive[27]. This provides some limits on the potential excesses inherent whenever unilateral retaliation is allowed under international law.

4. INVESTOR-STATE DISPUTE SETTLEMENT

The NAFTA contains an innovative system for the settlement of disputes between NAFTA investors and the government of another NAFTA Party. The NAFTA allows investors, on their own and on behalf of their investments, to claim against governments for the breach of the obligations of the NAFTA Investment chapter. Traditionally, the only actors capable of bringing international legal disputes have been states. However, the NAFTA changes this characteristic of international law by empowering a broadly-defined class of potential litigants through the investor-state dispute process.

The introduction of a process which allows for widespread individual access to dispute resolution is perhaps the single most significant legal development which has taken place through the NAFTA. The investor-state dispute settlement system has created a system of claim adjudication parallel to national courts. Under other international agreements, there were relatively few disputes raised as governments preferred to settle contentious issues privately. The NAFTA provides a process whereby a large number of disputes will be taken out of the realm of diplomatic consultations entirely and can be heard without governmental consent. Thus, individuals will have the ability to shape the jurisprudence of the NAFTA to a greater degree than under any other international agreement. This may well have significant implications for future international agreements.

NAFTA investors may seek both monetary damages as final judgment[28] and interim equitable orders[29]. These orders may be immediately enforceable under the terms of the *Washington Convention* or under the *New York Convention on the Recognition and Enforcement of Foreign Arbitral Awards*[30].

(a) WHO CAN BRING A CLAIM?

Only NAFTA nationals may bring investor-state claims. The NAFTA defines a national to be a person who is a citizen or a permanent resident of a Party[31]. Under the generally accepted international legal norms, inter-

---

27 NAFTA article 2019.
28 NAFTA article 1134.
29 NAFTA article 1135.
30 NAFTA article 2012.
31 NAFTA article 201.

national law could only be used to pursue the claims of foreigners against a host government. The NAFTA changes this by allowing a juridical national (*i.e.* a corporation) to use an international agreement to advance a claim against its own government. NAFTA article 1117(1) provides that:

> An investor of a Party, on behalf of an enterprise of another Party that is a juridical person that the investor owns or controls directly or indirectly, may submit to arbitration under this section a claim that the other Party has breached an obligation under:
> (a) Section A[32] or Article 1503(2) (State Enterprises), or
> (b) Article 1502(3)(a) (Monopolies and State Enterprises) where the monopoly has acted in a manner inconsistent with the Party's obligations under Section A,
> and that the enterprise has incurred loss or damage by reason of, or arising out of, that breach.

This gives an entitlement to a very large class of potential litigants. The only NAFTA investors who may not avail themselves of investor-state dispute settlements are those investors, or their controlled Mexican investments, who have initiated proceedings before Mexican courts[33]. In such a case, NAFTA investor-state dispute settlement is not available.

An investor of a NAFTA Party who owns, or controls a company in another NAFTA Party may bring a claim regarding the breach of a NAFTA obligation. Nowhere is it required that there be diversity of nationality between the enterprise bringing the claim and the government being claimed against. Thus, for example, it is possible for an American national to invest in Mexico through a controlled Mexican corporation. In this example, the American national will be able to bring a claim on behalf of the Mexican company against the Mexican government for a breach of NAFTA investment obligations, while a Mexican citizen would not be able to make such a claim.

Under general principles of international law, a national could have no standing to invoke international legal commitments against his/her own government. Under the NAFTA, a national acting directly may not do this either. However there appears to be no block to this indirect approach. Thus, in this example, the Mexican company would have acquired superior legal rights against its own government by using the NAFTA[34]. Accordingly, this NAFTA definition may result in significant developments in the application of the NAFTA to domestic circumstances.

---

32 Section A refers to the Investment chapter obligations other than dispute settlement.
33 NAFTA annex 1120.1(b).
34 This type of situation has been considered by a number of international tribunals. See, for example, the decision of the U.S.-Iran Claims Tribunal in *Esphahanian* v. *Bank Mellat*, 2 *Iran-U.S. Claims Tribunal Reports* 157.

(b) BRINGING A CLAIM

Claims may be brought by a NAFTA investor within three years of the time that the investor first had knowledge of the breach of the NAFTA obligation[35]. In addition, article 1118 suggests that the disputing parties "should" first attempt to settle a claim through consultation or negotiation.

Claimants are required to provide notice to the defendant government of their intent to claim at least 90 days before the claim is submitted[36]. This notice must provide basic information about the investor, the nature of the dispute including the facts, and the relief sought. If there are a number of claims which are based on a common question of fact or law, the tribunal can order the consolidation of the claims[37], or hear one of them as a representative claim[38].

Claims can be submitted under three different types of dispute rules. If the Party of the investor and the defending government are both members of the International Centre for the Settlement of Dispute (ICSID)[39], then the ICSID dispute rules will apply. If only one is a party to the ICSID, then the ICSID Additional Facility rules will apply[40]. If the Party of the investor and the defending government are not parties to the ICSID, then the arbitration rules of the United Nations Commission on International Trade Law (UNCITRAL) will apply[41]. When the NAFTA came into force, of the NAFTA Parties, only the United States was a party to the *Washington Convention*. While the procedural aspects of these three arbitral regimes are very similar, there are differences in how awards can be reviewed and enforced under each system.

Before a claim may be considered, the investor (and the investment if applicable) must agree to consent to the NAFTA investor-state arbitration rules and waive all other legal recourse other than that provided by the NAFTA[42]. If the claim is regarding the loss of corporate control of an enterprise, then the consent of that enterprise is not necessary[43].

---

35 NAFTA articles 116(2) and 1117(2).
36 NAFTA article 1119.
37 NAFTA article 1126(2)(a).
38 NAFTA article 1126(2)(b).
39 The ICSID was created by the *Washington Convention of 1965*, which is formally known as the *Convention on the Settlement of Investment Disputes between States and Nationals of Other States*, produced at Washington, Mar. 18, 1965, 575 U.N.T.S. 160 (1966).
40 ICSID document ICSID/11, June 11, 1979.
41 NAFTA article 1120. The UNCITRAL rules were adopted by the United Nations General Assembly on Dec. 15, 1976 as resolution 31/98. They are also reproduced at 15 I.L.M. 701 (1976).
42 NAFTA article 1121.
43 NAFTA article 1121(3).

Tribunals are comprised of three arbitrators: one is appointed by each litigant with the third appointed to preside, who is selected by agreement of the litigants. If one of the litigants refuses to appoint an arbitrator then the process will not be frustrated. The Secretary-General of the ICSID is authorized to appoint missing arbitrators if 90 days have elapsed without nomination by the litigant[44]. If the claims of many disputes are based on the same facts, the Secretary-General of the ICSID may consolidate the hearings together before one common panel[45].

(c) CHOICE OF LAW

NAFTA article 1131 gives investor-state tribunals the absolute right to determine issues based on the NAFTA itself and international law. If a Party relies on a reservation or exception in annexes I, II, III or IV, questions on its interpretation must be referred to the Free Trade Commission which has 60 days to provide a binding interpretation[46]. If no interpretation is presented, then the panel may make its own judgment. Otherwise, there is no provision for arbitral tribunals to seek an opinion from the Free Trade Commission on the interpretation of the NAFTA itself. The NAFTA does allow the Commission to make interpretations which would bind a tribunal[47]. As well, the NAFTA provides that a Party may address submissions to an investor-state tribunal on interpretative issues[48].

(d) AWARDS

An investor-state tribunal may make interim or final awards. Interim awards may include injunctive relief to preserve evidence or to protect the tribunal's jurisdiction[49]. Tribunals however, do not have the authority to order the seizure of a good or to strike down a measure that violates the NAFTA. In its final award, the tribunal may only award monetary damages, interest and restitution of property[50]. These awards are final and binding.

(e) ENFORCEMENT

Awards made under the ICSID rules can be enforced directly under the *Washington Convention*[51]. Awards made under the ICSID Additional Fa-

---

44   NAFTA article 1124.
45   NAFTA article 1126.
46   NAFTA article 1132.
47   NAFTA article 1131(2).
48   NAFTA article 1128.
49   NAFTA article 1134.
50   NAFTA article 1135. The tribunal may not award specific performance.
51   *Washington Convention* Article 53 states that "each Party shall abide by and comply with

cility or UNCITRAL however must be enforced under existing international conventions that deal with the enforcement of arbitral awards such as the *New York Convention*[52] or the *Panama Convention*[53].

The *New York Convention* is the preeminent international convention dealing with the recognition of international arbitral awards. Its general rule is that arbitral awards must be enforced within its signatory members. The *New York Convention* sets out five grounds on which an arbitral award may not be enforced. These are:

1. award was not made in the territory of a Party state[54];
2. subject matter of the dispute was not commercial in nature[55];
3. award must be binding in the country where it was made[56];
4. arbitrator was under some incapacity[57]; or
5. enforcement of the award would offend public policy[58].

Through its terms, the NAFTA has prohibited review of arbitral awards on the first three grounds[59], however, review of arbitral awards on the basis of arbitrator incapacity or offending public policy is still possible.

The NAFTA provides that investor-state arbitral awards can be enforced nothwithstanding the fact that a challenge to the enforcement of the award under section V of the *New York Convention* is taking place. Awards against Canada or the United States may be made public. Awards against Mexico will only be made public on the mutual agreement of both litigants[60].

(f) REVIEW OF AN ICSID AWARD

Article 53 of the *Washington Convention* states that an ICSID award is binding on the parties and not subject to appeal. However, the Convention does provide for three types of review:

---

the terms of an award". Article 54 states that "Parties will enforce an ICSID award as if it were a final judgment of a court of that state".

52 *United Nations Convention on the Recognition and Enforcement of Foreign Arbitral Awards,* signed at New York, June 10, 1958; 21 U.S.T. 2817, 330 U.N.T.S. 3.

53 More precisely, this is the *Inter-American Convention on International Commercial Arbitration,* signed Jan. 30, 1975.

54 *New York Convention* Article I(1).

55 *New York Convention* Article I(3).

56 *New York Convention* Article V(1)(3).

57 *New York Convention* Article V(i)(e).

58 *New York Convention* Article V(ii)(b).

59 For example, NAFTA article 1135(7) provides that the Parties agree that the subject matter of any dispute raised under the Agreement will be commercial in nature.

60 NAFTA annex 1137.4.

1. interpretation on the meaning of the award[61];
2. revision on the basis of the discovery of a previously unknown fact of decisive importance[62]; and
3. annulment by an ad-hoc committee[63].

Ad-hoc co   mittee review has been used by a number of ICSID litigants as a means of delaying the imposition of an award[64]. Article 52 of the *Washington Convention* provides that a party to an arbitration may request that an award be annulled on the basis of lack of jurisdiction, violation of due process and the failure to give reasons for an award. Annulment hearings are heard by an ad-hoc committee of three arbitrators who have the full power to annul all or part of the panel's award.

5. INVESTMENT DISPUTES REGARDING FINANCIAL SERVICES

The Canada-U.S. Free Trade Agreement did not allow for dispute resolution regarding its financial service obligations. The NAFTA specifically allows for dispute resolution on its financial service provisions. Disputes regarding the NAFTA Financial Services chapter can be handled by three different bodies: the Free Trade Commission, a state-to-state dispute settlement panel or a NAFTA investor-state dispute settlement tribunal.

The Free Trade Commission has authority to interpret the NAFTA and its annexes. If the Free Trade Commission is unable to agree on the interpretation, then a state-to-state dispute settlement panel can be established to interpret the NAFTA. When dealing with financial service issues, the Parties to the dispute may select a panel from a special roster of financial service experts[65]. Investor-state dispute settlement panels may also interpret the NAFTA when an interpretive question is raised in a dispute between a NAFTA investor and a Party. The areas upon which these disputes can be raised is limited to Investment chapter provisions which have been incorporated into the Financial Services chapter[66].

---

61 *Washington Convention* Article 50.
62 *Washington Convention* Article 51.
63 *Washington Convention* Article 52.
64 A more thorough discussion of this issue is provided in chapter 7 of Alan Redfern and Martin Hunter, *Law and Practice of International Commercial Arbitration* (2nd ed.) (London: Sweet & Maxwell, 1991) at 413.
65 NAFTA article 1414.
66 These provisions were inserted by NAFTA article 1401(2).

If a NAFTA investor-state dispute panel is convened in the area of financial services, special provisions have been added to give greater protection to the Parties from vexatious suits. All investor-state disputes dealing with financial services must go the Financial Services Committee first. The Committee has one specific authority: to determine whether, or to what extent the NAFTA prudential measures exception[67] provides a defence to the dispute. It has 60 days to decide this issue. If there is no answer within 60 days or no defence, the panel may proceed.

While these special provisions protect Parties from suits dealing with prudential measures[68] or interpretations of NAFTA annexes, apparently special provisions for NAFTA investor-state tribunal interpretations of the Agreement were not provided for[69]. If the Financial Services Committee finds that none or only part of the measure in dispute falls outside the prudential capacity of government, then the investor-state dispute tribunal will be convened.

If a state-to-state dispute occurs and the panel finds a measure to be inconsistent with a NAFTA Financial Service chapter obligation, the complaining Party may suspend benefits only in the financial service sector[70]. If the panel finds that there is an inconsistency but it is in another sector, a Party may not suspend benefits in the financial services sector[71].

---

67 NAFTA article 1410.
68 As defined by NAFTA article 1410.
69 Article 1414 provides that where a financial services provision goes to a chapter 20 dispute panel, a special panel of financial experts may be called upon. These rules do not apply to investor-state dispute settlement.
70 NAFTA article 1414(5)(b).
71 NAFTA article 1414(5)(c).

21

Exceptions and Reservations

Agreements such as the NAFTA impose very broad disciplines on governmental activity in a wide number of areas. This can result in limitations on existing government policies resulting in political, economic or social uneasiness for governments. As a result, the NAFTA provides for two methods by which policies, which would otherwise be inconsistent with the Agreement can be preserved[1]. Because of their similar ability to allow governments to insulate actions from their NAFTA obligations, exceptions and reservations are reviewed together.

1. EXCEPTIONS TO THE NAFTA

NAFTA chapter 21 contains detailed provisions which allow governments to follow policies that would otherwise be inconsistent with the NAFTA. Governments are not required to identify those policies that can take advantage of these exceptions until such time as the policies are challenged before a NAFTA dispute panel. At that time, if a Party can prove that it is relying on a *bona fide* exception, then that inconsistent policy can be maintained. In addition, there are a number of specific exceptions which are included within each NAFTA chapter. For example, in the Financial Services chapter there is an exception which allows governments to maintain otherwise inconsistent policies taken for prudential reasons[2]. Many of the NAFTA's exceptions are identical to those contained in the GATT and the Canada-U.S. Free Trade Agreement. These exceptions are as follows.

---

1 This is in addition to the NAFTA provisions on emergency actions, such as those in chapter 8, which allow Parties to temporarily suspend the application of certain obligations due to unforseen injury to domestic markets.
2 NAFTA article 1410.

(a) GATT EXCEPTIONS

The NAFTA incorporates the entire list of general exceptions provided for in GATT Article XX[3]. This provides some consistency in exclusions between the NAFTA and the GATT[4]. However, while the GATT exceptions are available throughout that Agreement, in the NAFTA, these incoporated the GATT exceptions only apply to NAFTA chapters 3 to 9. While the Agreement appears to grant an exception for services, it provides that a Party may only adopt measures that are consistent with the Agreement and that do not constitute a means of arbitrary discrimination between countries where the same conditions prevail or a disguised restriction on trade exists between the Parties[5]. This hardly qualifies as an exception at all. This results in having no GATT exceptions available for areas such as investment, services, telecommunications, government procurement, temporary entry of business persons and intellectual property. Only exceptions which occur in those chapters, or which are listed as permitted reservations will be allowed.

GATT Article XX allows a country to impose import or export controls that may otherwise be inconsistent with the obligations of the GATT, if the controls are not imposed in a manner that would constitute a means of arbitrary or unjustifiable discrimination between countries or a disguised restriction on international trade. The measures may be imposed for the following reasons:

(a) to protect public morals;
(b) to protect human, animal or plant life or health;
(c) to regulate trade in gold and silver;
(d) to secure compliance with domestic laws or regulations, not otherwise consistent with the GATT, such as the protection of intellectual property and the prevention of deceptive practices;
(e) to restrict or prohibit goods produced by prison labour;
(f) to protect national treasures of artistic, historic, or archaeological value;
(g) to achieve the conservation of exhaustible natural resources, if such measures are taken in conjunction with restrictions on domestic production or consumption;

---

3 NAFTA article 2101.
4 Although there are some differences in the commitments of Parties due to differences in their obligations under the Protocol on Provisional Application of the GATT which are not available under the NAFTA. Canada and the United States made their Protocols in 1947, while Mexico did not make its Protocol until Aug. 24, 1986; GATT, BISD, 33 Supp. 3.
5 NAFTA article 2101(2).

(h) to effect commodity agreements approved by members of the GATT; and

(i) to preserve certain commodities in short supply.

The GATT exceptions were examined during an interpretive dispute between Canada and the United States under the Canada-U.S. Free Trade Agreement. A chapter 18 panel was convened at the request of the United States to review the consistency of Canadian landing requirements for salmon and herring[6]. Canadian law required that all salmon and herring caught in Canadian waters had to be landed in Canada, so that statistical records could be maintained, before being exported. Canada argued that the measure was justified on the grounds that it related to Canada's ability to conserve an exhaustible natural resource and as such was excepted by GATT Article XX(g).

The panel did not agree entirely with the Canadian position. It found that the requirement that 100 percent of the catch be landed in Canada was not necessary to achieve the goal of conservation. The measure was not "primarily aimed" at Canadian management of the resource. The panel did uphold the right of Canada to take measures to protect its fisheries through data collection but this landing requirement went too far[7]. The dispute was ended after the panel decision with a negotiated settlement between the Parties.

This decision under the Canada-U.S. Free Trade Agreement should give a strong indication of how the same provisions would be interpreted under the NAFTA. Under the earlier agreement, exception clauses have been interpreted narrowly. The panel established that a government can take measures aimed at protecting their resources if the measure is primarily aimed at protection. At the same time, the panel suggested that there must be some sense of proportionality taken in the measure to relate the trade-distortion against the objective of the measure.

The NAFTA clarifies that measures to "protect human, animal or plant life or health" include both environmental measures and measures relating to "the conservation of exhaustible natural resources" including the conservation of living and non-living natural resources[8]. This wording is broader than the GATT exception. However, it will likely not be capable of being interpreted to allow Parties to discriminate between goods based on their production process rather than by the type of good[9].

---

6 *In the Matter of Canada's Landing Requirement for Pacific Salmon and Herring*, CDA 89-1807-01 (U.S.-Canada Binational Panel, Oct. 16, 1989).

7 *Salmon and Herring case*, at 51-52.

8 NAFTA article 2101(2).

9 This was the issue at the centre of the GATT Panel Decision on U.S. Restriction on Imports of Tuna decided Aug. 16, 1991, 30 I.L.M. 1594. This panel ruled that the *Marine*

(b) NATIONAL SECURITY INTERESTS

Nothing in the Agreement affects the ability of a NAFTA Party to take measures necessary for the protection of its essential security interests relating to its military or nuclear weapons, or matters undertaken in pursuit of United Nations Charter obligations for peace and security[10].

(c) TAXATION POLICY

The NAFTA does not apply to taxation measures other than the specific ones set out in the Agreement, such as export taxes[11]. In the case of inconsistency between the NAFTA and a bilateral tax convention, the applicable double tax convention will prevail to the extent of the inconsistency[12]. The exception also details provisions regarding allowable direct and indirect taxes in a number of areas.

For example, NAFTA provisions which prohibit export taxes and national treatment for imports will apply to existing and future tax measures regarding trade in goods[13]. National treatment will also continue to apply to some capital and all income taxes, regarding the purchase or consumption of services. Other specified tax rules will also be unable to be exempted from the national treatment requirements in the Agreement.

Governments may not rely on this NAFTA exception to avoid the prohibition on imposing certain performance requirements in connection with the receipt of a tax advantage[14]. As well, the NAFTA investment provisions dealing with expropriation will apply to taxation measures, but before an investor can raise a claim, the investor must have the "competent authorities"[15] determine whether the measure is an expropriation or not[16].

(d) BALANCE OF PAYMENTS

NAFTA article 2104 permits the Parties to apply trade restrictions to counteract serious balance of payment difficulties. The article is subject to

---

Mammal Protection Act, 16 U.S.C. §§1361-1407 (1988), which prohibited the sale of tuna in the United States by companies caught using practices harmful to dolphins, was contrary to American GATT obligations as the criteria for discrimination was not based on the product (tuna) but on the process (non-dolphin-safe nets).

10 NAFTA article 2102.
11 NAFTA article 2103.
12 *Canada-U.S. Tax Convention*, 1980 and the *U.S.-Mexican Tax Convention*, 1992.
13 NAFTA article 2103(3).
14 NAFTA article 2103(5).
15 These are set out in NAFTA annex 2103.6.
16 NAFTA article 2103(6).

a number of exceptions and mandates that measures be in accordance with the provisions of the International Monetary Fund.

2. RESERVATIONS

Reservations to international treaties allow governments to exempt specific areas from the operation of a treaty. In this way, "non-conforming measures" are permitted to continue. Reservations may only be made to treaties in a form agreeable to its signatories, which is usually specified in the text of the Agreement itself.

The NAFTA establishes a process whereby governments can list areas in which the Agreement will not apply. The NAFTA reservation process requires that there be a listing of measures within the NAFTA annexes at a specified time (for example, on the entry of the Agreement into force). If an area is not listed in the appropriate annex, then it will be incapable of being protected by the reservation.

There are two different types of reservations permitted under the NAFTA: bound and unbound. Each of these confers a different type of policy room for the applicable government. Bound reservations permit a government to maintain an existing measure which does not conform to a NAFTA obligation. Governments are allowed the ability to amend these measures in future, but never in a way that is more trade distorting. The type of government acts that can be reserved is exceedingly broad as the NAFTA defines the term "measures" to include "laws, regulations, procedures, requirements or practices"[17].

Unbound reservations differ from bound ones in two ways. They permit governments to not only maintain the existing non-conforming measures, but they may make new ones in the future. Also, they do not refer to any specific measure, but to entire broad sectors of the economy. Thus there is a much greater ability for governments to take future action under unbound reservations than bound ones.

(a) WHO CAN MAKE RESERVATIONS?

Reservations may only be made by the NAFTA Parties on their own behalf as well as on behalf of state and provincial governments. Annexes I and VII set out bound reservations by federal, state and provincial governments regarding specific measures which would otherwise be inconsistent with the Investment, Services and Financial Services chapters. Annex V sets out existing quantitative restrictions maintained by the NAFTA Par-

---

17 NAFTA article 201.

ties[18]. National government reservations to annexes I, V and VII were completed at the time of the signature of the NAFTA. While further national reservations are not possible, significant numbers of reservations on behalf of subnational governments can be made to these annexes as set out in the NAFTA.

Annex II describes sectors in which governments have retained the right to maintain existing non-conforming measures and adopt new measures relating to investment and services. These reserved measures include:

- aboriginal affairs[19];
- residency requirements attached to the ownership of oceanfront land[20];
- telecommunication transport networks and services, radiocommunications and submarine cables (*i.e.* "basic" telecommunication services)[21];
- minority affairs[22]; and
- law enforcement[23].

The annex II reservations permit broad policy making within their listed sectors.

(b) SUBNATIONAL "RESERVATIONS" TO THE NAFTA

The NAFTA provides for the listing of certain existing non-conforming state and provincial measures in annexes I, V and VII of the Agreement. Subnationals are unable to add to the list of exempt unbound measures in annex II.

The exact form that reservations must take is specified in the opening terms of each annex (known as "the chapeau" of the annex). Parties have two years from the date of implementation (January 1, 1996) to make

---

18 NAFTA article 1207 requires that federal measures be listed in the NAFTA on its signature. Provincial and state measures are to be listed by Jan. 1, 1995.

19 NAFTA annex II, Schedule of Canada at II-C-1, NAFTA annex II, Schedule of the United States at II-U-6.

20 NAFTA annex II, Schedule of Canada at II-C-2, NAFTA annex II, Schedule of the United States at II-U-1.

21 NAFTA annex II, Schedule of Canada at II-C-3 and II-C-5, NAFTA annex II, Schedule of Mexico at II-M-4, NAFTA annex II, Schedule of the United States at II-U-2.

22 NAFTA annex II, Schedule of Canada at II-C-8, NAFTA annex II, Schedule of Mexico at II-M-9, NAFTA annex II, Schedule of the United States at II-U-6.

23 NAFTA annex II, Schedule of Canada at II-C-9, NAFTA annex II, Schedule of Mexico at II-M-11, NAFTA annex II, Schedule of the United States at II-U-5. This reservation is discussed more fully in chapter 11 of this book.

reservations against obligations contained in the Investment and Cross-Border Trade in Services chapters. Reservations to the Financial Services chapter from all Canadian subnationals and the states of California, Florida, Illinois, New York, Ohio and Texas were required by January 1, 1994. Other American states have until January 1, 1995 to list their financial service reservations. Reservations of existing quantitative measures are due on January 1, 1995.

Reservations may be taken against only certain NAFTA obligations which are set out in the following table.

Investment	Services	Financial Services
• National Treatment	• National Treatment	• National Treatment
• Most-Favoured-Nation Status	• Most-Favoured-Nation Status	• Most-Favoured-Nation Status
• Performance Requirements	• Local Presence Obligations	• Establishment of Financial Institutions
• Senior Management and Boards of Directors		• Senior Management and Boards of Directors
		• Regulation of Cross-Border Trade
		• New Financial Services and Data Processing

The Financial Services chapter provides the greatest capacity for reservation. Not only does it have the greatest number of obligations to which reservations can be made, it also contains the "prudential exception" which insulates many measures from the application of the Agreement. Thus, the obligations imposed upon governments by the Financial Services chapter is significantly lesser than a first reading of the chapter might suggest[24].

---

24 It should be noted that only non-conforming measures can be listed in annex VII. Thus, a measure which is listed in annex VII would usually not be capable of being considered exempt under the prudential exception, which covers measures which, by definition, are NAFTA-consistent.

(i) Considerations before listing a reservation

Before a subnational government reserves a measure under the NAFTA, there are three fundamental questions which must be carefully considered. They are as follows.

1. *Is the measure existing?*

    - Only existing measures can be reserved by subnationals under the NAFTA[25]. "Existing" refers to the time that the NAFTA came into force. Accordingly, if a measure was not existing on January 1, 1994, a reservation cannot be made.

    - The NAFTA defines the term "measures" to include "laws, regulations, procedures, requirements or practices"[26]. It is simple to establish the existence of laws and regulations at a given time, but there can be evidential difficulties in establishing whether a procedure, requirement or practice was actually in existence at the time the NAFTA came into force.

2. *Is the measure inconsistent with the NAFTA obligation?*

    - Only inconsistent measures can be listed. If a measure does not conflict with the NAFTA, then it cannot be reserved. Thus, measures which are exempt due to a NAFTA exception or measures which can be preserved through the financial services prudential exception may not qualify for listing as reservations. In addition, it is important to name the appropriate NAFTA obligation. For example, many issues are on the border between being a financial service or a cross-border service. Placing a reservation against the wrong NAFTA obligation could make the reservation ineffective.

3. *Is the NAFTA obligation one that can be reserved against?*

    - Reservation is only allowed against a small number of NAFTA obligations. If the measure infringes a NAFTA obligation that permits reservation, then a reservation could be made. If no reservation is permitted, then there is no way to preserve the inconsistent measure.

    - A second consideration is timing. Once the NAFTA reservation deadlines are completed, there is no way to add an additional reservation without amending the NAFTA. Thus, a Canadian sub-

---

25 This is set out in NAFTA articles 1108(1)(a), 1206(1)(a) and 1409(1)(a).
26 NAFTA article 201.

national could not add a financial service reservation to annex VII as it is past the deadline of January 1, 1994.

(ii) The Interpretation of Reservations

No understanding of the NAFTA reservation process can be complete without a review of how reservations are interpreted. The reservations build upon each other, and upon the NAFTA exceptions, to undo what the NAFTA purports to do. This creates a tension within the document between the goal of trade liberalization, on one hand, and the competing goal of maintaining effective government policy tools, on the other. These competing goals are likely to lead to disputes. NAFTA investors may find that their views, on the meaning of a certain NAFTA provision differ greatly from that of a government. Thus, being able to quickly and efficiently deal with interpretive issues is important to the operation of the NAFTA.

NAFTA reservations will be interpreted by either NAFTA dispute panels (in the case of a chapter 20 dispute) or the Free Trade Commission (in the case of an investor-state dispute)[27]. Within the chapeau of most NAFTA annexes is a detailed set of provisions which specify how reservations should be listed and interpreted. Each reservation is divided into a number of sections dealing with issues such as: the sector involved, the duration of the reservation (phase-out), the type of NAFTA obligation reserved against, the measure involved (if applicable) and the description. When interpreting a reservation, all elements of the reservation will be considered[28]. For annex II reservations, in the case of ambiguity, the description element will prevail[29]. For annexes I and VII, the following interpretative hierarchy occurs:

1. The phase-out element will prevail over all other inconsistent elements.
2. If there is no inconsistency with the phase-out, then one looks to the measure element as modified by the description.
3. If the measure is not qualified by the description, then the measure alone will prevail unless[30]:

> any discrepancy between the Measures element and the other elements considered in their totality is so substantial and material that it would be unreasonable to conclude that the Measures element should prevail. . . .

---

27 NAFTA article 1132.
28 NAFTA annexes I(3), II(3), VII(3).
29 NAFTA annex II(3).
30 NAFTA annexes I(3), VII(3).

This hierarchy is somewhat perplexing as one must look to a reasonable standard if the measure is not modified by a description. If the measure is modified by a description, then apparently no reasonableness need be exhibited in the interpretation of the measure.

These general rules will be interpreted in light of the NAFTA objective to "expand and enhance the benefits of this Agreement"[31]. In addition, annex 1404.4 provides that the Parties will consult on the further liberalization of cross-border trade in financial services no later than January 1, 2000.

---

31 NAFTA article 102.

22
Final Provisions

The NAFTA's final chapter deals with issues such as adding new members to the trade agreement, withdrawing from the agreement and changing it.

1. ACCESSION

By design, the NAFTA was created not to be a trilateral agreement, but a multilateral framework document[1]. It provides that any country or groups of countries may join the Agreement subject to any terms agreed to by the new member and the Free Trade Commission[2]. Since all decisions of the Free Trade Commission are taken by consensus[3], this suggests that unanimity is required before a new member can join the Agreement. However, article 2204(2) provides that if a Party does not consent to the new member, that Party may declare that the NAFTA will not apply between it and the new member.

It is interesting to note that there is no geographical limitation on the countries that can join. New members do not have to be from North America, or the Western hemisphere. This is a clear difference from other international agreements, like the Treaty of Rome which limited membership in the European Union only to European States[4].

A number of countries, and groups of countries, have expressed an interest in seeking membership to the NAFTA. Thus, any ambiguities contained within these NAFTA articles are likely to be resolved by the Parties.

The NAFTA also appears to contemplate the ability for there to be overlapping trade agreements between its members and non-Parties. The Agreement contains a clause which allows its Parties to enter into other agreements with other countries.

---

1 Other than chapter 7 which sets out two bilateral agricultural deals, all the NAFTA chapters are capable of being the basis of a multilateral agreement of wide application.
2 NAFTA article 2204(1).
3 NAFTA article 2001(4).
4 *Treaty of Rome*, article 237.

2. WITHDRAWAL

Any Party may withdraw from the NAFTA on six-months notice to the other Parties. The withdrawal of a Party does not terminate the NAFTA, which continues to be in force with its other remaining Parties[5].

3. AMENDMENT

The NAFTA may be amended at any time by its Parties. Any modification of the NAFTA must be approved in accordance with the applicable legal procedures in each Party[6] and would constitute an integral part of the agreement[7].

---

5 NAFTA article 2205.
6 NAFTA article 2202(2). This raises an interesting question on how the NAFTA could be amended by the United States. The NAFTA is an executive agreement and as such could conceivably be amended by Presidential authority notwithstanding that it has been approved by Congress. This question remains open.
7 NAFTA article 2202.

23

Interpretation of the NAFTA

1. NAFTA OBJECTIVES

The NAFTA sets out clear rules for its interpretation. Like all international treaties, it is subject to the international jurisprudence on treaty interpretation. However, in response to earlier Canada-U.S. Free Trade Agreement panel decisions which relied upon international interpretive rules, the NAFTA negotiators established priority interpretive provisions in article 102 to ensure that the NAFTA will be interpreted in accordance with its objectives[1]. The NAFTA objectives suggest that the NAFTA provisions will be interpreted broadly. The NAFTA objectives are to:

(1)   (a)   eliminate barriers to trade in, and facilitate the cross-border movement of, goods and services between the territories of the Parties;

      (b)   promote conditions of fair competition in the free trade area;

      (c)   increase substantially investment opportunities in the territories of the Parties;

      (d)   provide adequate and effective protection and enforcement of intellectual property rights in each Party's territory;

      (e)   create effective procedures for the implementation and application of this Agreement, for its joint administration and for the resolution of disputes; and

      (f)   establish a framework for further trilateral, regional and multilateral cooperation to expand and enhance the benefits of this Agreement.

(2)   The Parties shall interpret and apply the provisions of this Agreement in the light of its objectives set out in paragraph 1 and in accordance with applicable rules of international law.

The NAFTA's interpretive article shows some resemblance to the interpretive wording contained in chapter 1 of the Canada-U.S. Free Trade Agreement. The intentions underlying the NAFTA's wording can be better understood by reviewing the development of interpretive issues under the Canada-U.S. Free Trade Agreement. Interpretive disputes under the Canada-U.S. Free Trade Agreement were handled by chapter 18 panels. For

---

1   The NAFTA rules take priority because of NAFTA article 103(2) which mandates that the NAFTA takes precedence over other international agreements. This section also indicates the clear unambiguous intention of the Parties and thus under standard interpretive rules, should govern the interpretation of the Agreement.

example, a Canada-U.S. Free Trade Agreement binational dispute panel ruled on the interpretation of that agreement's rules of origin regarding the amortization of automotive machinery[2]. In making its decision, the panel followed the rules of treaty interpretation contained in the *Vienna Convention on the Law of Treaties*[3] that treaties are to be interpreted in accordance with their ordinary meaning.

Unlike the practice in common law jurisdictions, there is no recognition of precedent[4] in international law. Thus, the decisions of other international bodies, or even the International Court of Justice do not provide judgments which are binding upon future international arbitrators. However, earlier international decisions have persuasive force for future tribunals and often play a role like precedent in the common law system.

The NAFTA mandates that its objectives be looked to when the Agreement is being interpreted. This marks a textual change from the Canada-U.S. Free Trade Agreement, perhaps in response to the decisions of panels made under that agreement. As a result, one should expect future NAFTA interpretations to take into account not only the *Vienna Convention* provisions on treaty interpretation but also the specifics of article 102.

While NAFTA article 102 takes priority over international law in the interpretation of the NAFTA, it does not insulate the NAFTA from international law. It simply makes clear that its future interpreters should follow its objectives in arriving at its interpretation. With this in mind, interpreters are free to look to the "applicable rules of international law".

2. APPLICABLE RULES OF INTERNATIONAL LAW ON INTERPRETATION

The process of treaty interpretation is complex and inherently difficult. The first principle of international treaty interpretation is that words will be looked to in their ordinary meaning wherever possible. In the words of the International Court of Justice[5]:

> the Court considers it necessary to say that the first duty of a tribunal which is called upon to interpret and apply the provisions of a treaty, is to endeavour to give effect to them in their natural and ordinary meaning in the context in which they occur. If the relevant words in their natural and ordinary meaning make sense in their context, that is an end of the matter.

2 *In the Matter of Article 304 and the Definition of Direct Cost of Processing or Direct Cost of Assembling*, USA-92-1807-01. (Canada-U.S. Binational Panel, June 8, 1992). The final decision is reported at 57 FR 46,502 (1992).

3 U.N. Doc. A/Conf 39-27, May 23, 1969.

4 That is usually referred to as the principle of *stare decisis*.

5 *Competence of the General Assembly for the Admission of a State to the U.N.*, also known as the *Second Admissions case*, I.C.J. Reports (1948) at 8.

This point is also reflected in the *Vienna Convention on the Law of Treaties*, which codified the international law on treaty interpretation. Article 31 of this Convention provides that a treaty will be interpreted in its "ordinary meaning ... in their context and in light of its object and purpose".

Interpreters may then look at the preambles and annexes of a treaty. While these may not form a part of the technical treaty, they provide important context for interpreters[6]. The preamble to the NAFTA sets out a number of trade liberalizing goals, including: commitments for economic growth, competitiveness, secure markets, conservation, and basic workers' rights within the North American market. While these commitments are not binding in themselves, they provide important context to NAFTA interpreters.

Besides looking at the terms of a treaty, interpreters may also look to other documents. With the implementation of the NAFTA, the American and Canadian governments issued statements which indicate their unilateral interpretation of the NAFTA. There is no provision in the *Vienna Convention*, or international law itself, that provides that the unilateral statements of any treaty Party may be used to give a binding interpretation of a treaty obligation. However *Vienna Convention* article 31(2) does allow that a treaty be interpreted in its context which can include:

b)   any instrument which was made by one of more parties in connexion with the conclusion of the treaty and accepted by the other parties as an instrument related to the treaty.

The American *Statement of Administrative Action* and the Canadian *Statement of Government Action* are instruments made by the Parties "in connexion with the conclusion of the treaty". There is no indication that these documents have been accepted by the other NAFTA Parties as an instrument related to the treaty, so that their interpretive weight is somewhat questionable.

There are other documents which can also have an influence on how a treaty is interpreted. *Vienna Convention* article 31(3) allows interpreters to take into account letters exchanged after the conclusion of agreements. These letters are taken into account in establishing the context of the treaty. In themselves, they do not have the capacity to re-write the treaty unless the letters themselves purport to do that. These letters may only be relied on when a panel or tribunal decides that the simple meaning of the NAFTA

---

6 NAFTA article 2201 specifies that the NAFTA annexes form an integral part of the Agreement. Since there is no mention of the Preamble forming a part of the Agreement, the *Vienna Convention* will govern how the Preamble may be used as an interpretive tool.

provision was unclear. For if there is no lack of clarity apparent to the panel, then no interpretation need take place[7].

Finally, article 32 of the *Vienna Convention* permits one to look at materials indicating the intention of the negotiators as a supplementary means only if the meaning after following article 31 is ambiguous, obscure or manifestly unreasonable[8].

---

7 The binational panel decision on the interpretation of article 304 provides an example where a trade panel decided that it was unnecessary to use rules of interpretation for the simple meaning of the words was clear.

8 While the *Vienna Convention* provides that one can look to the "preparatory work of a treaty", there is no publicly available access to the *travaux préparatoires* of the NAFTA. All that is available are notes which are contained in the NAFTA and its annexes.

24

Supplemental Agreements to the NAFTA on Environmental and Labour Cooperation

On September 14, 1993, Canada, Mexico and the United States agreed to two agreements supplementing the NAFTA on the issues of Labour and Environmental Cooperation. The principal goal of these agreements was to address concerns over the domestic enforcement of environmental and labour laws.

These agreements refer to the general obligations of the NAFTA Parties to provide fair treatment and enforcement of their labour and environmental laws. The Supplemental Agreements do not speak to the establishment of any specific levels of environmental or labour protection. The application of these agreements is further narrowed by the definition of laws and regulations in each agreement. For example, the North American Agreement on Labour Cooperation only permits dispute settlement on the relatively narrow basis of whether a Party has persistently failed to enforce its domestic laws and regulations relating to occupational health and safety or other technical labour standards[1].

1. THE NORTH AMERICAN AGREEMENT ON ENVIRONMENTAL COOPERATION

The North American Agreement on Environmental Cooperation provides that its Parties will observe general environmental and procedural principals and adequately enforce its own national laws. The key commitment of the Environmental Supplemental Agreement is that Parties will ensure that their environmental laws and regulations provide for "high

---

1 NAFTA Labour Supplemental Agreement article 23(2). Technical labour standards are defined in article 49 to exclude child labour and child minimum-wage measures.

levels of environmental protections"[2]. At the same time, NAFTA Parties have recognized their rights to establish their own levels of domestic environmental protection and to modify them accordingly. Nothing in the agreement requires Parties to harmonize their standards in an upward fashion.

Parties must provide that persons with a legally-recognized interest have appropriate access to the administrative, quasi-judicial and judicial tribunals for the enforcement of that Party's environmental laws[3]. Each Party must provide in its laws that there will be procedures to remedy violations of its environmental laws[4]. However, the North American Agreement on Environmental Cooperation narrowly defines "environmental law or regulation" to mean a law or regulation to protect the environment or health and safety relating only to emissions of pollutants, control of toxic substances and the protection of wild flora and fauna[5]. There is no provision that would require a remedy for violations of other environmental laws[6]. Parties are also required to provide procedural guarantees that their administrative, quasi-judicial and judicial proceedings are fair, equitable and transparent[7]. This commitment includes the provision of reasons for decisions which must be in writing[8]. Parties must also ensure that their laws include access to injunctions.

(a) ADMINISTRATIVE STRUCTURE

The NAFTA Environmental Supplemental Agreement is administered through a Commission for Environmental Cooperation (the Environmental Commission) headed by a Council of Ministers and assisted by a Secretariat and a Joint Public Advisory Committee[9].

(i) The Council

The Council is the governing body of the Environmental Commission. It oversees the implementation of the North American Agreement on

---

2 NAFTA Environmental Supplemental Agreement article 3.
3 NAFTA Environmental Supplemental Agreement article 6(2).
4 NAFTA Environmental Supplemental Agreement article 5(2).
5 NAFTA Environmental Supplemental Agreement article 45(2)(a). This definition only applies to public actions taken for enforcement in article 14 or articles 22-26.
6 Such as laws dealing with natural resource management or the conservation of flora and fauna.
7 NAFTA Environmental Supplemental Agreement article 7(2).
8 NAFTA Environmental Supplemental Agreement article 7(2).
9 NAFTA Environmental Supplemental Agreement article 8.

Environmental Cooperation and the work of its Secretariat[10]. It has the ability to "address" the interpretation of the Environmental Agreement[11] and to set the budgets and programs of the Environmental Commission.

The Council is similar in structure to its sibling, the Council established in the Labour Agreement, and to the NAFTA Free Trade Commission. It is comprised of Cabinet-level representatives of each Party[12]. It must meet annually in regular session and may meet in special session at the request of any Party[13]. All regular sessions must include public meetings. Other meetings held during regular or special sessions may be open to the public at the discretion of the Council[14]. All decisions of the Council are made on the basis of consensus except for those relating to the Secretariat or dispute settlement[15].

The Council may consider and develop recommendations regarding a large number of areas. These include, but are not restricted to the following[16]:

- comparability of methodology for data gathering;
- pollution prevention techniques;
- approaches for reporting on the state of the environment;
- use of economic instruments for the pursuit of environmental objectives;
- scientific research and technology development in respect of environmental matters;
- promotion of public awareness regarding the environment;
- transboundry and border environmental issues;
- exotic species that may be harmful;
- conservation of wild flora and fauna;
- protection of endangered and threatened species;
- environmental emergency preparedness;
- environmental matters as they relate to economic development;
- environmental implications of goods throughout their lifecycles;
- human resource training and development in the environmental field;

---

10 NAFTA Environmental Supplemental Agreement article 10(1).
11 NAFTA Environmental Supplemental Agreement article 10(1)(d). This is not the same as giving the Commission the power to give binding interpretations of the Supplemental Agreement.
12 NAFTA Environmental Supplemental Agreement article 9(1).
13 NAFTA Environmental Supplemental Agreement article 9(3)(b).
14 NAFTA Environmental Supplemental Agreement article 9(4).
15 NAFTA Environmental Supplemental Agreement article 9(6). The areas subject to a two-thirds vote are the staffing of the Secretariat (11(2)); the preparation of special reports by the Secretariat (13(1)); the revision of Secretariat reports (21(2)); and requests for a panel (24).
16 NAFTA Environmental Supplemental Agreement article 10(2).

- exchange of environmental scientists and officials;
- approaches to environmental compliance and enforcement;
- ecologically-sensitive national accounts; and
- eco-labelling.

The Council is required to cooperate with the Free Trade Commission to achieve the environmental goals and objectives of the NAFTA by:

(a) Acting as a point of inquiry and receipt for comments of Non-Governmental Organizations.

(b) Providing assistance in consultations made regarding the observation by a Party of NAFTA article 1114 which deals with the lowering of environmental, health or safety standards to attract investment.

(c) Contributing to the prevention on environment-related trade disputes under the NAFTA by making recommendations to the Free Trade Commission on avoiding disputes[17] and identifying experts able to provide information on NAFTA committees, working groups and other bodies.

(ii) The Secretariat

The Environmental Supplemental Agreement creates a Secretariat for the Environmental Commission, which will be based in Montréal, Québec. The Secretariat provides technical, administrative and operational support to the Council and the agreement's other committees[18]. It also is responsible for drafting the Annual Report of the Commission which must be made public[19].

At the direction of a two-thirds vote of the Council, the Secretariat may prepare a report on any environmental matter related to the cooperative functions of the agreement[20]. This report may not deal with questions related to whether a Party has failed to enforce its own environmental laws and regulations[21]. The Secretariat may also receive submissions from any Non-Governmental Organization or any person alleging the non-enforcement of environmental laws and regulations of a NAFTA Party[22]. The Secretariat has the discretion to determine if the complaint "merits request-

---

17 NAFTA Environmental Supplemental Agreement article 10(6)(c).
18 NAFTA Environmental Supplemental Agreement article 11(5).
19 NAFTA Environmental Supplemental Agreement article 12.
20 NAFTA Environmental Supplemental Agreement article 13(1).
21 This is the basis for dispute settlement under this agreement and may only be raised by the Parties.
22 NAFTA Environmental Supplemental Agreement article 14(1).

ing a response from the Party". This determination is made on the basis of the following criteria[23]:

(a) the submission alleges harm to the person or organization making the submission;

(b) the submission, alone or in combination with other submissions, raises matters whose further study in this process would advance the goals of this Agreement;

(c) private remedies available under the Party's law have been pursued; and

(d) the submission is drawn exclusively from mass media reports.

The specific consideration of whether the submission is drawn exclusively from mass media reports merits some attention. Article 14(2)(d) suggests that the fact that a complaint is based solely on mass media reports is relevant in assessing whether the complaint merits requesting a reply. This section does not say whether extra credibility or caution is to be applied for mass media reports.

If the Secretariat believes that there is merit in requesting a response from a Party, the submission of a complainant will be forwarded to that Party. After the submission is forwarded, the Party has 30 days to respond[24]. If the Secretariat believes that the Party's response warrants further action, it may inform the Council. The Council may, by a two-thirds vote, order that a factual record be prepared[25]. A draft factual record will be submitted to the Council when it is completed. Any Party may comment on the accuracy of the draft report within 45 days[26]. These comments, if appropriate, will be incorporated into the final record and then be submitted to the Council. The Council may, by a two-thirds vote, make the final factual record public within 60 days[27].

(iii) Advisory Committees

The Environmental Supplemental Agreement creates public advisory committees to advise each Party and the Council. Each Party will appoint members to its National Advisory Committee. The Party, or its National Advisory Committee, will appoint members to the Joint Public Advisory Committee (JPAC)[28]. The JPAC is required to receive, at the same time as

---

23 NAFTA Environmental Supplemental Agreement article 14(2).

24 NAFTA Environmental Supplemental Agreement article 14(3). A party has 60 days to respond in exceptional circumstances.

25 NAFTA Environmental Supplemental Agreement article 15.

26 NAFTA Environmental Supplemental Agreement article 15(5).

27 NAFTA Environmental Supplemental Agreement article 15(7).

28 NAFTA Environmental Supplemental Agreement article 17.

the Council, drafts of annual programs and budgets, the annual report and all other reports prepared by the Secretariat other than factual records[29]. The Council may make available factual records prepared by the Secretariat available to the JPAC[30]. Parties may also create government committees comprised of members of national and subnational governments to assist them in implementing the agreement[31].

(b) DISPUTE SETTLEMENT

Individuals have no right of action under the Environmental Supplemental Agreement. Only national governments may initiate disputes. The only basis for such a dispute can be a claim regarding a NAFTA Party's persistent pattern of non-enforcement of its own environmental laws[32].

The Supplemental Agreement attempts to settle disputes through consultations wherever possible[33]. If the Parties cannot settle the dispute after 60 days of discussions, then a special session of the Council will be convened[34]. The Council may make recommendations which can be made public. If the matter has not been resolved within 60 days, the Council may, by a two-thirds vote, commence an arbitral panel. A panel of five panelists will be chosen from a roster of 45 eligible individuals[35] who have expertise in environmental law or in the resolution of international disputes or other relevant experience[36]. The question that panels will consider is "the matter where the alleged persistent pattern of failure to effectively enforce its environmental law relates to a situation involving workplaces, firms, companies or sectors that produce goods or provide services:

a)   traded between the territories of the Parties; or
b)   that compete in the territory of the Party complained against, with goods or services produced or provided by persons of another Party"[37]

Other NAFTA Parties with a substantial interest in the complaint may appear before the panel as a complaining Party if they make their intention known by the seventh day after the creation of the panel[38].

---

29 NAFTA Environmental Supplemental Agreement article 16(4).
30 NAFTA Environmental Supplemental Agreement article 16(7).
31 NAFTA Environmental Supplemental Agreement article 18.
32 These terms are given more meaning by the NAFTA Environmental Supplemental Agreement article 45(1). They are discussed in more detail in chapter 25 of this book.
33 NAFTA Environmental Supplemental Agreement article 22.
34 NAFTA Environmental Supplemental Agreement article 23(1).
35 NAFTA Environmental Supplemental Agreement article 25(1).
36 NAFTA Environmental Supplemental Agreement article 25(2).
37 NAFTA Environmental Supplemental Agreement article 24(1).
38 NAFTA Environmental Supplemental Agreement article 24(2).

The Supplemental Agreement establishes a complicated set of deadlines for the preparation of panel reports. Panel reports may include findings, determinations and recommendations. A panel is required to submit its draft report to the disputing Parties within 60 days[39]. The Parties then have 30 days to submit their comments on the report to the panel[40]. The panel then must present the final report to the Parties within 60 days of presenting the initial report[41]. This final report must be transmitted, along with any comments from the disputing Parties, to the Council within 15 days. Once a final report has been transmitted to the Council, it must be made public within five days[42].

If the panel finds a persistent pattern of failure to enforce environmental laws, the Parties are required to agree on a mutually-satisfactory action plan to conform with the panel report[43]. If the Parties cannot agree on an action plan or if implementation of the agreed upon action plan does not occur, the panel may be reconvened[44]. Action by a Party on the failure to implement an action plan may not occur sooner than 180 days after the action plan was agreed upon[45]. This matter itself may be the subject of a further panel[46].

If the Parties cannot agree on an action plan, the panel which heard the dispute may be reconvened to determine an action plan and to impose a fine[47].

If the Parties cannot agree on whether an action plan is being effectively implemented, the panel may be reconvened. In this case, if the panel finds that the action plan is not being implemented, then the panel must impose a fine[48]. Where the panel finds that its report has not been implemented by the offending Party, it may impose a fine of up to US $20 million for 1994 and up to 0.007 percent of total bilateral trade in goods in subsequent years[49]. Fines would be channelled to a fund to be used for environmental enforcement.

If the action plan imposed by a reconvened panel is not implemented within 180 days, then the panel may be reconvened again[50]. If a fine ordered

---

39 NAFTA Environmental Supplemental Agreement article 32(1).
40 NAFTA Environmental Supplemental Agreement article 31(4).
41 NAFTA Environmental Supplemental Agreement article 32(1) unless the Parties otherwise agree.
42 NAFTA Environmental Supplemental Agreement article 32.
43 NAFTA Environmental Supplemental Agreement article 33.
44 NAFTA Environmental Supplemental Agreement article 34.
45 NAFTA Environmental Supplemental Agreement article 34(3).
46 NAFTA Environmental Supplemental Agreement article 35.
47 NAFTA Environmental Supplemental Agreement article 34(4).
48 NAFTA Environmental Supplemental Agreement article 34(5)(b).
49 NAFTA Environmental Supplemental Agreement annex 34.
50 NAFTA Environmental Supplemental Agreement article 35.

by a panel is not paid within 180 days, then the complaining Party may retaliate by withdrawing equivalent NAFTA benefits from the non-compliant Party[51]. Annex 36B sets out limitations on how trade retaliation can be taken. For example, the annex provides that retaliation should first be taken in the same sector as the persistent failure to enforce environmental law[52].

Because of its concerns over the effects of trade retaliation, a special enforcement regime applies to awards against Canada. Annex 36A provides that trade retaliation may not occur against Canada. Instead, Canada has modified its domestic laws to make any monetary award by an Environmental Supplemental Agreement panel directly enforceable in Canada as if it were the order of a Canadian court[53].

2. THE NORTH AMERICAN AGREEMENT ON LABOUR COOPERATION

The North American Agreement on Labour Cooperation was created to deal with concerns that the creation of a free trade zone between developed and developing states could lead to significant competitive pressures to lower labour standards. While similar in structure to the Environmental Supplemental Agreement, the Labour Agreement speaks more to general principles. Parties are obliged to ensure that their labour laws and regulations provide for "high labour standards consistent with high quality and productivity workplaces and shall continue to strive to improve those standards in that light"[54].

(a) OBLIGATIONS UNDER NATIONAL LAW

Parties must provide that persons with a legally-recognized interest have appropriate access to administrative, quasi-judicial, judicial and labour tribunals for the enforcement of that Party's labour laws. Each Party must provide in its laws that persons will have recourse to procedures to protect their rights under its labour laws[55] and collective agreements[56].

Parties are required to provide procedural guarantees that their administrative, quasi-judicial, judicial and labour proceedings are fair, equitable and transparent, including the provision of written reasons for decisions[57].

---

51 NAFTA Environmental Supplemental Agreement article 36.
52 NAFTA Environmental Supplemental Agreement annex 36B(2)(a).
53 *Crown Liability and Proceedings Act*, S.C. 1994, ss. 20.1, 20.2.
54 NAFTA Labour Supplemental Agreement article 2.
55 Including occupational safety and health, employment standards, industrial relations and migrant workers.
56 NAFTA Labour Supplemental Agreement article 4.
57 NAFTA Labour Supplemental Agreement article 5(2).

The decisions of these tribunals are not subject to review under the terms of the Labour Supplemental Agreement[58].

In addition, the Parties are obligated to promote, to the maximum extent possible, the following guiding principles[59]:

- freedom of association and the right to organize;
- right to collective bargaining;
- right to strike;
- prohibition of forced labour;
- labour protection for children and young persons;
- minimum employment standards;
- elimination of employment discrimination;
- equal pay for men and women;
- prevention of occupational accidents and diseases;
- compensation for occupational injuries and illnesses; and
- protection of migrant workers.

Parties must ensure that their labour laws and regulations provide for "high labour standards consistent with high quality and productivity workplaces and shall continue to strive to improve those standards in that light"[60]. The Supplemental Agreement does not contain any commitment upon the Parties to harmonize their standards in an upward fashion. Parties are similarly not obligated to make their standards compatible although they do agree to cooperate in this area[61].

Parties are obligated to provide appropriate access to judicial, administrative or labour tribunals for the domestic enforcement of labour rights and domestic laws. The North American Agreement on Labour Cooperation defines "labour law or regulation" as meaning only laws and regulations directly related to[62]:

- freedom of association and protection of the right to organize;
- right to bargain collectively;
- right to strike;
- prohibition of forced labour;
- labour protection for children and young persons;

---

58 NAFTA Labour Supplemental Agreement article 5(8).
59 NAFTA Labour Supplemental Agreement annex 1.
60 NAFTA Labour Supplemental Agreement article 2.
61 For example, article 11(3) of the NAFTA Labour Supplemental Agreement provides that when the Council is carrying out cooperative labour activities, it is to pay "due regard" to the economic, social, cultural and legislative differences between them.
62 NAFTA Labour Supplemental Agreement article 49.

- minimum employment standards, such as minimum wages and over-time pay, covering wage earners, including those not covered by collective agreements;
- elimination of employment discrimination on the basis of grounds such as race, religion, age, sex or other grounds as determined by each Party's domestic laws;
- equal pay for men and women;
- prevention of occupational injuries and illnesses;
- compensation in cases of occupational injuries and illnesses; and
- protection of migrant workers.

(b) ADMINISTRATIVE STRUCTURE

The NAFTA Labour Supplemental Agreement is administered through a Commission for Labour Cooperation (the Labour Commission) which is comprised of a Council, a Secretariat and is assisted by a National Administrative Office in each Party[63].

(i) The Council

The Council is the governing body of the Labour Commission. It oversees the implementation of the North American Agreement on Labour Cooperation and the work of its Secretariat[64]. It has the ability to "address" the interpretation of the Labour Agreement[65] and to set the budgets and programs of the Labour Commission.

Like the Environmental Council, the Labour Council is comprised of Cabinet-level representatives of each Party[66]. It must meet annually in regular session and may meet in special session on the request of any Party[67]. All regular sessions must include public meetings and other meetings held during regular or special sessions may be open to the public at the discretion of the Council[68]. All decisions of the Council are made on the basis of consensus except as otherwise provided by the Supplemental Agreement.

---

63 NAFTA Labour Supplemental Agreement article 8.
64 NAFTA Labour Supplemental Agreement article 10(1).
65 NAFTA Labour Supplemental Agreement article 10(1)(g). This is identical to article 10(1)(d) in the Environmental Supplemental Agreement.
66 NAFTA Labour Supplemental Agreement article 9(1).
67 NAFTA Labour Supplemental Agreement article 9(3)(b).
68 NAFTA Labour Supplemental Agreement article 9(4).

(ii) The Secretariat

The Labour Supplemental Agreement creates a Secretariat for the Labour Commission, which will be based in Dallas, Texas, to support the Council and the agreement's other committees[69]. It also is responsible for drafting the Annual Report of the Commission which must be made public[70]. The Secretariat is mandated to make periodic background reports setting out publicly-available information supplied by each Party on[71]:

(a) labour law and administrative procedures;
(b) trends and administrative strategies related to the implementation and enforcement of labour law;
(c) labour market conditions such as employment rates, average wages and labour productivity; and
(d) human resource development issues such as training and adjustment programs.

It should be noted that this broad mandate is somewhat reduced by a rather restrictive definition to the term "publicly-available information". It is defined to only apply to "information to which the public has a right to know under the statutory laws of the Party"[72]. Thus, information which could be protected on the basis of litigation or executive privilege could not form the basis of any Secretariat reports.

At the direction of the Council, the Secretariat may prepare a study on any matter[73]. This report will be made public within 45 days of its submission to the Council unless the Council otherwise orders. Unlike the Secretariat of the Environmental Commission, the Labour Secretariat does not have any role in the investigation or resolution of labour-enforcement issues.

The Supplemental Agreement establishes National Administrative Offices (NAO) within each country. The roles of National Administrative Offices are to assist the Secretariat serve as a contact point within each Party and to serve as a focus for consultations and cooperative activities among the Parties[74]. Parties may create National Advisory Committees and Government Committees. National Advisory Committees are comprised of members of the public, including representatives of business and labour, to advise Parties on the implementation and elaboration of the agreement[75]. A Government Committee may be created in each Party comprised of mem-

---

69 NAFTA Labour Supplemental Agreement article 13.
70 NAFTA Labour Supplemental Agreement article 13(c).
71 NAFTA Labour Supplemental Agreement article 14(1).
72 NAFTA Labour Supplemental Agreement article 49.
73 NAFTA Labour Supplemental Agreement article 14(1).
74 NAFTA Labour Supplemental Agreement article 16.
75 NAFTA Labour Supplemental Agreement article 17.

bers of national and subnational governments to assist in implementing the agreement[76].

(c) CONSULTATION AND REPORTS

Parties are obliged to seek cooperation and consultation in resolving matters in dispute. Consultations can occur through the National Administrative Offices of each Party or through Ministerial consultations. If a matter has not been resolved through consultations, then any consulting Party may request that the Council establish an Evaluation Committee of Experts (ECE)[77]. An ECE may only review the patterns of practice of each Party in the enforcement of its occupational safety and health or other technical matters. A Party may contest the establishment of an ECE on the grounds that the matter is not trade-related, or it is covered by mutually-recognized labour laws. In such a case, the Council will appoint an expert who will rule on this issue within 15 days[78].

A mutually-recognized labour law is defined as a labour law of the petitioning Party which addresses the same general subject matter as the law of the other Party[79]. These provisions would have the effect of limiting the scope of enforcement challenges to situations where trade is directly affected and would prevent challenges by Parties who have no equivalent laws of their own. In the case of a finding of non-enforcement, a successful challenge under the dispute-settlement mechanism must demonstrate a pattern of practice of violations. Such a pattern must include a series of events which occurred after January 1, 1994, and does not arise from a single instance or case[80].

(d) PANELS

After a final ECE report that establishes that a Party is not enforcing its labour law has been presented to the Council, consultations between the Parties may start again. If these consultations are unsuccessful after 60 days, then a Party may require the holding of a special session of the Council[81]. If the dispute still has not been settled within 60 days after the

---

76 NAFTA Labour Supplemental Agreement article 18. A government committee is particularly important for Canada where most labour regulation is under provincial jurisdiction.

77 NAFTA Labour Supplemental Agreement article 23(1).

78 NAFTA Labour Supplemental Agreement annex 23.

79 NAFTA Labour Supplemental Agreement article 49.

80 NAFTA Labour Supplemental Agreement article 49.

81 NAFTA Labour Supplemental Agreement article 28.

Council has met, then, on the written request of a Party and a two-thirds vote, a dispute panel will be created.

A panel comprised of five panelists will be chosen from a roster of 45 eligible individuals[82] who have expertise in labour law or in the resolution of international disputes or other relevant experience[83]. Panel reports may include findings, determinations that there has been a persistent lack of enforcement of labour standards and recommendations. A panel is required to submit its draft report to the disputing Parties within 180 days[84]. The Parties then have 30 days to submit their comments on the report to the panel[85]. The panel must present the final report to the Parties within 60 days of presenting the initial report[86]. This final report must be transmitted, along with any comments from the disputing Parties, to the Council within 15 days. Once a final report has been transmitted to the Council, it must be made public within five days.

If the panel finds a persistent pattern of failure to enforce labour laws, the Parties may agree on a mutually-satisfactory action plan to conform with the panel report[87]. If the Parties cannot agree on an action plan, or if implementation of the agreed upon action plan does not occur, the panel may be reconvened[88]. Action by a Party on the failure to implement an action plan may not occur sooner than 60 days and no later than 120 days after the action plan was agreed upon[89].

If the Parties cannot agree on an action plan, the panel which heard the dispute may be reconvened to determine an action plan and to impose a fine[90].

If the Parties cannot agree on whether an action plan is being effectively implemented, the panel may be reconvened. In this case, if the panel finds that the action plan is not being implemented, then the panel must impose a fine[91]. Where the panel finds that its report has not been implemented by the offending Party, it may impose a fine of up to US $20 million for 1994 and up to 0.007 percent of total bilateral trade in goods in subsequent years. If the action plan imposed by a reconvened panel is not implemented within 180 days, then the panel will be reconvened. If a fine ordered by a panel is

---

82 NAFTA Labour Supplemental Agreement article 30.
83 NAFTA Labour Supplemental Agreement article 32.
84 NAFTA Labour Supplemental Agreement article 36(2).
85 NAFTA Labour Supplemental Agreement article 36(4).
86 NAFTA Labour Supplemental Agreement article 37.
87 NAFTA Labour Supplemental Agreement article 38.
88 NAFTA Labour Supplemental Agreement article 39.
89 NAFTA Labour Supplemental Agreement article 39(2).
90 NAFTA Labour Supplemental Agreement article 39(4)(b).
91 NAFTA Labour Supplemental Agreement article 39(5)(b).

not paid within 180 days, then the complaining Party may retaliate by withdrawing equivalent NAFTA benefits from the non-compliant Party[92]. As with enforcement of fines under the Environmental Supplemental Agreement, a special enforcement regime applies to awards against Canada under this agreement. Annex 31A provides that trade retaliation may not occur against Canada. Instead, Canada has modified its domestic laws to make any monetary award by a Supplemental Agreement panel immediately enforceable in Canada as if it were the order of a Canadian court[93].

3. IMPLICATIONS OF THE LABOUR AND ENVIRONMENTAL AGREEMENTS FOR SUBNATIONALS

State and provincial governments provide a significant amount of environmental legislation in Canada and the United States, but they are not Parties to the NAFTA or its Supplemental Agreements. This is a particular concern in Canada given its constitutional division of powers that does not provide its federal government the full authority to implement international agreements that affect its provinces[94].

(a) THE ENVIRONMENTAL AGREEMENT

The Environmental Supplemental Agreement provides that its terms only apply to those provinces which are listed by the government of Canada. Annex 41 sets out how the dispute settlement provisions affect Canada. Unless a certain threshold of participating provinces is met, Canada may only initiate disputes in areas that are within the federal jurisdiction of Canada. The threshold for the Environmental Agreement is set at the listing of provinces that account for at least 55 percent of Canada's gross domestic product[95]. Table 1 sets out the gross domestic product of Canada's provinces. In addition to these general thresholds, the agreements provide that at least 55 percent of the total production in an industry involved in a dispute must also be from participating provinces[96].

(b) THE LABOUR AGREEMENT

Similarly, the Labour Supplemental Agreement provides that its terms only apply to those provinces which are listed by the government of

---

92 NAFTA Labour Supplemental Agreement article 41.

93 *Crown Liability and Proceedings Act*, S.C. 1994, ss. 20.1, 20.2.

94 This issue is more fully discussed in chapter 2 of this book.

95 NAFTA Environmental Supplemental Agreement annex 41(4)(b).

96 NAFTA Environmental Supplemental Agreement annex 41(4)(c).

Canada. Annex 41A sets out how the dispute settlement provisions affect Canada. Until a certain threshold of participating provinces is met, Canada may only initiate disputes in areas that are within the federal jurisdiction of Canada. The threshold for the Labour Supplemental Agreement is the inclusion of the federal government and provinces which must account for at least 35 percent of Canada's labour force[97]. Table 2 sets out the breakdown of the labour force of Canada's provinces. In addition to these general thresholds, the agreements provide that at least 55 percent of the workers in the concerned industry must be employed in a participating province[98].

Provinces that have not joined the agreement may not initiate or benefit from consultations or dispute proceedings. In addition, Canada may only initiate dispute settlement against another Party if the non-enforcement relates to matters that, within Canada, would be under federal jurisdiction. Under both Supplemental Agreements, Canada may amend the lists of covered provinces at any time upon six-months notice[99].

Table 1

PROVINCIAL GDP, 1992 (at market prices)

	$ Millions	**% Share**
Canada	684,184	100.0
Newfoundland	9,368	1.4
Prince Edward Island	2,126	0.3
Nova Scotia	18,004	2.6
New Brunswick	13,910	2.0
Québec	158,296	23.1
Ontario	275,421	40.3
Manitoba	23,751	3.5
Saskatchewan	19,837	2.9
Alberta	73,744	10.8
British Columbia	86,571	12.7
Yukon Territory	1,014	0.1
Northwest Territories	2,142	0.3

Source: Statistics Canada (Catalogue 13-213)

---

97 NAFTA Labour Supplemental Agreement annex 46(4)(b).
98 NAFTA Labour Supplemental Agreement annex 46(4)(c).
99 NAFTA Labour Supplemental Agreement annex 46(1) and NAFTA Environmental Supplemental Agreement annex 41(1).

Table 2

PROVINCIAL LABOUR FORCE, 1992
(not including the Yukon Territory or the Northwest Territories)

	000's	% Share
Canada	13,796	100.0
Newfoundland	236	1.7
Prince Edward Island	64	0.5
Nova Scotia	416	3.0
New Brunswick	331	2.4
Quebec	3,385	24.5
Ontario	5,286	38.3
Manitoba	535	3.9
Saskatchewan	480	3.5
Alberta	1,370	9.9
British Columbia	1,693	12.3

Source: Statistics Canada (Catalogue 71-220)

25

Frequently-Raised Concerns on the NAFTA

1. CULTURAL INDUSTRIES

International trade agreements can have a significant effect in liberalizing trade in cultural products, but also can pose significant threats to national cultural sovereignty. As a result, a number of countries, notably France in the Uruguay Round GATT negotiations and Canada in the NAFTA, have sought exemptions for their cultural industries from international trade commitments. Concern over the effects of trade agreements regarding cultural industries has been a long-standing Canadian concern. Perhaps this concern is heightened by the proximity of Canada's audience of 18 million English-speaking persons to the immense American cultural market. Whatever the basis for the concerns, many Canadians have questioned whether the NAFTA actually exempts Canadian culture from the Agreement.

Concern over cultural sovereignty was an important domestic consideration for the Canadian negotiators of the Canada-U.S. Free Trade Agreement. Commenting on the issue of culture and the Canada-U.S. Free Trade Agreement, S.M. Lipset identified the concerns of those Canadians who fear bilateral free trade. He wrote[1]:

> what they fear is, that their country will be flooded in American cultural products, and that the distinct character of its intellectual output will be lost in the much larger, more affluent and more aggressive society to the south. Some also worry that Canada will become in effect or in reality, the 51st American state.

As a result of these fears, the final text of that Agreement contained provisions which provided for an exemption of cultural industries from the application of most of the trade Agreement's obligations. The definition of cultural industries covers five different types of activity[2]:

---

1 S.M. Lipset, *Continental Divide: The values and institutions of the United States and Canada.* (New York: Routledge, 1990.) at 5.
2 Canada-U.S. Free Trade Agreement article 2012.

- printed publications;
- film and video;
- music recording;
- music publishing; and
- broadcasting.

On these activities, there is an exemption for Canada-U.S. Free Trade Agreement Party governments. Article 2005 states:

> 1. Cultural industries are exempt from the provisions of this agreement, except as specifically provided in Article 401 (Tariff Elimination), paragraph 4 of Article 1607 (divestiture of an indirect acquisition) and Articles 2006 and 2007[3] of this Chapter.

> 2. Notwithstanding any other provision of this Agreement, a Party may take measures of equivalent commercial effect in response to actions that would have been inconsistent with this Agreement but for paragraph 1.

By its terms, this exemption has two elements. First, paragraph 1 provides that cultural industries will be exempt from the operation of that agreement other than in specified circumstances. Paragraph 2 provides that a Party may retaliate against the use of the cultural exemption by taking actions of "equivalent commercial effect". It is the retaliation provision which has caused the most attention. Unlike other exemptions in trade agreements, the cultural exemption in the Canada-U.S. Free Trade Agreement fails to provide any protection from retaliation for relying upon the exemption itself. This is a rather unusual arrangement.

The NAFTA does not include provisions in its text regarding cultural industries. Instead, NAFTA annex 2106 incorporates the provisions of the Canada-U.S. Free Trade Agreement directly into the NAFTA text. Thus, the benefits and peculiarities of the cultural exemption have been continued into the later Agreement.

Within its NAFTA implementation legislation, Congress has put the Canadian government on notice that it will be carefully monitoring Canadian actions. The implementing Act contains a requirement that the United States Trade Representative will look out for any act, policy or practice that is adopted by the government of Canada that affects American cultural industries[4].

The NAFTA has not assuaged the concern of Canadian cultural providers that the NAFTA could have harmful effects upon Canadian culture. Given the political sensitivity of this issue in Canada, the Canadian government included a statement on culture in its *Statement of Government*

---

3 These articles detailed obligations regarding retransmission rights and print-in-Canada publishing requirements.

4 *North American Free Trade Agreement Implementation Act* §513.

Action. The statement essentially agrees that the United States has the ability to retaliate against the Canadian use of its cultural industries exemption. It states[5]:

> while the cultural industries' exemption has been retained and applies in respect of any Canadian cultural industry, the U.S. right to retaliate is limited to measures inconsistent with the FTA, not the NAFTA and therefore cannot be exercised with respect to new areas covered by NAFTA such as intellectual property.

While this statement is essentially correct, it fails to mention that NAFTA Parties have also denied themselves the opportunity to seek review of measures taken as equivalent commercial effect before the NAFTA Free Trade Commission, as otherwise provided for in the NAFTA. This is a significant limitation for a Party which is concerned about the threat of retaliation.

In addition to the cultural exemption, Canada has also maintained the ability to review all foreign investment in its cultural sector. Mexico has also reserved measures dealing with network and cable television programming. The rights and obligations between Canada and Mexico regarding cultural industries are identical to those applying between Canada and the United States.

(a) CONCLUSION

While the NAFTA contains a cultural industries exemption, its effect may be seen to be more diplomatic in nature than legal. Since the exemption does not protect a Party from retaliation for relying upon it, it provides little actual protection for a Party's cultural industries.

2. THE ENVIRONMENT AND THE NAFTA

The NAFTA is the first international trade agreement to deal with substantive environmental issues. Concerns over environmental policy are a relatively new matter for trade agreements. Before the negotiation of the NAFTA, trade agreements only incidentally touched on environmental matters. Usually, this was focused on narrow questions such as whether a technical standard was a necessary health measure or a disguised restriction on trade[6].

The NAFTA refers to the environment in a number of its chapters. Through these references, and its Supplemental Agreement which is dedi-

---

5 *Canada Gazette* Part I, Jan. 1, 1994 at 218-219.
6 For example, see GATT Articles XX(b) and XX(g).

cated to trade-related environmental matters, the NAFTA has crystallized the underlying links between trade agreements and the environment. This is not to suggest that the NAFTA adequately deals with environmental issues; the NAFTA is not an agreement which was designed to be "green" in any other way than to reflect the colour of money. The NAFTA is a mercantile agreement with incidental reference to the environment. While other trade agreements make limited mention of the environment, the NAFTA and its Environmental Supplemental Agreement makes its environmental links clear.

(a) CONGRESSIONAL PRESSURE TO MAKE NAFTA GREEN

In the United States, the 1991 GATT Panel decision on the *Marine Mammal Protection Act*, which ruled against American restrictions on tuna caught using non-dolphin-friendly nets, had an impact on focusing Congressional attention on the growing interdependence between trade and the environment. When President Bush sought extension to the Congressional Fast Track authority for the NAFTA in 1991, Congress imposed environmental objectives on the President. Once again, the interconnection between trade and the environment became clear when President Clinton, in order to increase support for the NAFTA in Congress, negotiated a Supplemental Agreement to the NAFTA focused primarily on ensuring adequate enforcement of domestic environmental regulations in each NAFTA Party.

(b) THE NAFTA AND THE ENVIRONMENT

The NAFTA itself does not contain any particular chapter on environmental measures. Instead, it contains provisions throughout its 22 chapters which deal with the environment. In particular, the Agreement deals with the environment in six areas:

i   Preamble;
ii   relationship with other agreements;
iii Sanitary and Phytosanitary Measures sub-chapter (chapter 7B);
iv   Technical Barriers to Trade chapter (chapter 9);
v   Investment chapter; and
vi   dispute resolution provisions.

The NAFTA does not address issues such as the enforcement of domestic environmental laws or issues of transboundry pollution. These concerns are canvassed in the Environmental Supplemental Agreement.

(i) Preamble

Among the 15 items listed in the NAFTA Preamble, two relate to the environment. The Preamble contains a statement that the Parties are committed to sustainable development and to strengthening the development of environmental laws and regulations. It should be noted that the objectives of the NAFTA contained in article 102 do not reflect either of these environmental goals. The NAFTA objectives are to be used as a basis for interpreting the NAFTA. Under international rules of treaty interpretation, while the Preamble may be looked at, it can only serve as a secondary interpretative vehicle in cases where there is definitional ambiguity.

(ii) Relationship with International Environmental Agreements

The NAFTA states that its terms will take priority over all other international agreements[7]. There is only one exception to this general rule. The NAFTA provides that five international environmental agreements will take priority in the case of an inconsistency between the agreements[8]. The NAFTA provides that where a Party has a choice among equally-effective and reasonably-available means of complying with such obligations, the Party must choose the alternative that is the least inconsistent with the other provisions of this Agreement[9]. In addition, the NAFTA allows its Parties to modify the list of environmental and conservation agreements which take precedence over the NAFTA[10].

(iii) Sanitary and Phytosanitary Measures

The setting of product standards is an important area of national environmental regulation. The NAFTA contains an entire sub-chapter dealing with sanitary and phytosanitary (SPS) measures, that is, measures taken for human, animal or plant life or health. The NAFTA recognizes the right of each Party to establish and apply its own levels of SPS measures[11]. Parties may take measures to protect human health and the environment but cannot use standards as disguised restrictions on trade. SPS measures may only be applied to the extent necessary to achieve the appropriate level of protection[12].

---

7 NAFTA article 103(2).
8 NAFTA article 104.
9 NAFTA article 104.
10 NAFTA article 104(2).
11 NAFTA article 712(1).
12 NAFTA article 712(5).

The NAFTA encourages harmonization based on international standards[13]. A Party's SPS measure that conforms to an international standard will be presumed to be consistent with the NAFTA SPS obligations[14]. This imposes a strong incentive on a Party to accept harmonization based on international standards. If the international standard is lower than the domestic standard, this could be a compelling force towards downward harmonization. However, if the domestic standard provides less health protection than the international one, then the NAFTA would equally compel upward harmonization of standards.

The NAFTA permits the sanitary and phytosanitary measures of other Parties to be treated as equivalent if they can be shown to meet the domestic level of protection[15]. It also encourages the Parties to pursue equivalence in SPS standards to the greatest extent practicable[16].

(iv) Technical Barriers to Trade

The NAFTA chapter on technical barriers to trade encourages harmonization of standards between the Parties. The Agreement suggests that international standards may serve as a basis for harmonization[17] and that if a Party uses an international standard as its own, that standard will be presumed to be consistent with the NAFTA technical barrier obligations[18]. While the NAFTA allows a Party to impose technical standards which are more stringent than the international standard[19], these measures may be challenged by another Party if they constitute an unnecessary barrier to trade[20].

Each NAFTA Party is entitled to maintain its own standards to determine its own levels of acceptable risk[21] for its "legitimate objectives" of human, animal or plant life or health, the environment or consumers[22]. In pursuing these legitimate objectives, Parties are to base their decisions on a number of criteria, including environmental conditions[23].

---

13 NAFTA article 712(1).
14 NAFTA article 713(2).
15 NAFTA article 714.
16 NAFTA article 713(5).
17 NAFTA article 905.
18 NAFTA article 905(2).
19 NAFTA article 905(3).
20 NAFTA article 904(4).
21 NAFTA articles 904(2) and 907.
22 NAFTA article 907(2).
23 NAFTA article 907(1)(d).

(v) Investment Provisions

The NAFTA attempts to address concerns that governments could engage in competitive social dumping, that is attracting investment by lowering their health, safety or environmental standards or enforcement. The NAFTA addresses this issue by recognizing the "inappropriateness" of encouraging investment by relaxing these protective measures[24]. Parties have agreed that they "should not" reduce, or offer to reduce, these measures as an encouragement for the establishment, acquisition, expansion or retention of investment. While this commitment is a significant diplomatic recognition of the importance of these standards, it does not constitute a binding legal commitment for the wording is conditional and not mandatory[25].

The NAFTA also acknowledges that investment considerations can have a negative impact on environmental standards. This concern is addressed primarily through article 1114. It provides that Parties may adopt, maintain and enforce any measure, consistent with the obligations of the Investment chapter, to ensure that investment activity is undertaken in a manner sensitive to environmental concerns[26].

These provisions regarding investment and the environment mark the first time that an international investment agreement has linked environmental and trade policy. However, while these provisions indicate a positive change in the sensitivity of trade agreements, they do not create any binding commitment on governments to maintain high levels of environmental, health or safety standards.

(vi) Environmental Dispute Settlement

The NAFTA's general procedure for dispute settlement is available for environmental disputes raised under the Agreement. As in all NAFTA disputes, there is a general obligation to consult before any other formal NAFTA dispute resolution process is initiated[27]. The failure to reach consensus could lead to either a NAFTA dispute panel or an investor-state dispute tribunal being convened.

(A) *The Forum*

NAFTA disputes may be settled under either the GATT or the NAFTA procedures except in two circumstances:

---

24 NAFTA article 1114(2).
25 For the commitment to be binding, it would have to use a term such as "a Party may not".
26 NAFTA article 1114(1).
27 NAFTA article 2006(5).

    i)   disputes regarding the consistency of the NAFTA with the identified environmental agreements in article 104[28]; or

    ii) standards disputes where the responding Party so requests[29].

In these circumstances, only the NAFTA dispute settlement is permitted.

The NAFTA requires that disputing Parties make a choice of which system they are going to use to settle their dispute. It is not possible to use both systems at the same time. Once a choice has been made, only that procedure may be used to settle the dispute.

Almost all environmental disputes which could be brought under the NAFTA between its Parties will be heard by a chapter 20 dispute panel. However, the failure of a Party to comply with NAFTA article 1114, which attempts to prevent social dumping, could lead to individual investors bringing an investor-state dispute.

(B) *Procedural Issues*

The NAFTA gives a procedural advantage to governments that wish to justify the legitimacy of their SPS measures. A NAFTA Party that challenges the NAFTA-consistency of a SPS measure has the burden of establishing the inconsistency[30]. This is a change in the burden of proof that is required under other international trade agreements such as the GATT or the Canada-U.S. Free Trade Agreement. This changed burden of proof is also available for the technical barriers to trade measures in the NAFTA[31].

The NAFTA makes it easier to bring scientific and environmental expert evidence before trade dispute panels. In the area of environmental dispute settlement, panels are likely to avail themselves to access of experts on any issue[32] or to scientific review boards on any factual issue concerning the environment, health, safety or other scientific matters in dispute[33]. Panels are required to take account of the reports from these sources[34].

(C) *Dispute Resolution*

If a NAFTA Party believes that another Party has engaged in policies which would violate the standards provisions or the social dumping provi-

---

28 NAFTA article 2005(3).

29 NAFTA article 2005(4).

30 NAFTA article 723(6).

31 NAFTA article 914(4).

32 NAFTA article 2014. This can only occur if the Parties to the dispute consent to the experts.

33 NAFTA article 2015. Scientific Review Boards can be appointed at the request of any disputing Party or on the initiative of the panel.

34 NAFTA article 2015(4).

sion in article 1114, then these matters could be the subject of consultations before the Free Trade Commission. The NAFTA Environmental Supplemental Agreement provides that these consultations should be assisted by the Council of the Commission for Environmental Cooperation[35]. The Council may also generally provide information or recommend experts to assist the Free Trade Commission on environmental disputes[36]. If these consultations do not resolve the dispute, then a dispute settlement panel can be struck. While NAFTA dispute panels do not have the power to strike down laws, or to compel environmental enforcement, they can lead to trade retaliation if appropriate action is not taken.

The NAFTA provides several enhancements to deal with disputes regarding standards issues. The NAFTA allows disputes to be raised before a NAFTA panel based on the application of the SPS or Technical Barriers to Trade chapter. In these areas, the required pre-panel consultations, may occur through expert committees created by the NAFTA[37].

(c) NAFTA ENVIRONMENTAL SUPPLEMENTAL AGREEMENT

The Environmental Supplemental Agreement contains a number of enhancements to the environmental issues covered by the NAFTA. The Environmental Supplemental Agreement creates a process which allows governments to take action on the non-enforcement of domestic environmental law by another Party. It does not entail significant rights for individual access. Although there is scope for public complaints to be made to the Secretariat concerning the persistent non-enforcement of environmental laws, the dispute settlement procedure can only be initiated by the Council. Furthermore, the Environmental Supplemental Agreement provides that there can be no private actions to compel enforcement of the terms of that agreement[38].

Environmental dispute resolution under the Supplemental Agreement can only occur in the following ways.

(i) Fact Finding

The Council may order that the Secretariat prepare a factual record based on the persistent non-enforcement of environmental laws. This re-

---

35 NAFTA Environmental Supplemental Agreement article 10(6)(b).
36 NAFTA Environmental Supplemental Agreement article 10(6)(c)(iii).
37 NAFTA articles 722 and 913. The Committee on Sanitary and Phytosanitary Measures and the Technical Barriers Committee are the appropriate bodies.
38 NAFTA Environmental Supplemental Agreement article 38.

quest to prepare a factual record can only originate from the Council, but it can be based upon complaints sent by the public, which have been investigated by the Secretariat.

(ii) Dispute Resolution

Dispute settlement under the Environmental Supplemental Agreement may only be initiated by national governments. The only basis for a dispute can be claims regarding a NAFTA Party's persistent patterns of non-enforcement of its own environmental laws. The term "persistent pattern" is defined by the agreement to mean a sustained failure occurring after January 1, 1994 to enforce environmental measures[39]. This definition is augmented by the following wording[40]:

> Party has not failed to "effectively enforce its environmental law". . . where the action or inaction in question by agencies or officials of that Party:
>
> (a) reflects a reasonable exercise of their discretion in respect of investigatory, prosecutorial, regulatory or compliance matters; or
>
> (b) results from *bona fide* decisions to allocate resources to enforcement in respect of other environmental matters determined to have higher priorities.

The Supplemental Agreement fails to give any meaning to the terms "reasonable exercise of discretion" or what constitutes a *bona fide* decision to allocate resources. What is clear is that this additional wording has significantly narrowed the scope of panel review for environmental non-enforcement under the Supplemental Agreement.

The Supplemental Agreement attempts to settle disputes through consultations wherever possible[41]. If the Parties cannot settle the dispute after 60 days of discussions, then a special session of the Council will be convened[42]. The Council may make recommendations which can be made public.

(iii) Enforcement

Where a panel finds that its report has not been implemented by the offending Party, it may impose a fine of up to US $20 million for the first year of the agreement and 0.007 percent of total bilateral trade in goods in subsequent years. If fines are not paid, the United States and Mexico have

---

39 NAFTA Environmental Supplemental Agreement article 45.
40 NAFTA Environmental Supplemental Agreement article 45.
41 NAFTA Environmental Supplemental Agreement article 22.
42 NAFTA Environmental Supplemental Agreement article 23(1).

agreed that trade retaliation could be imposed by the complaining country. Canada is exempt from trade retaliation. Instead, Canada has modified its domestic law[43] to permit the American and Mexican governments to enforce any fine as if it were the order of a Canadian court.

(d) PRODUCTION PROCESS STANDARDS AND THE NAFTA

Since the GATT panel decision on the *Marine Mammal Protection Act*, the legitimacy of production process standards has been at the centre of the debate over the interaction of trade and the environment[44]. The GATT permits important differentiation on the basis of product rather than by process. The American tuna measure was ruled inconsistent with GATT obligations because it only restricted imports of tuna that were caught using non-dolphin-friendly means. If the United States banned all tuna, then its measure would likely have been upheld by the GATT panel. Advocates of allowing process standards for imports suggest that trade law should be flexible enough to accomodate valid environmental concerns regarding how a good is produced. Detractors raise concerns that environmental process standards could become significant new trade barriers in themselves.

The NAFTA does not address the issue of production processes within its text. Not addressing the issue did not mean that the issue was not raised in the NAFTA debate. According to Lori Wallach of Public Citizen, the NAFTA's failure to deal with process standards will result in risk to a number of American laws which currently regulate product processes. In testimony to the Senate Finance Committee, she identified the following NAFTA-inconsistent laws: The *Marine Mammal Protection Act*, the *High Seas Driftnet Enforcement Act*, the *Sea Turtle Act*, the *Wild Bird Conservation Act*, the *Humane Slaughter Act*, the *African Elephant Conservation Act* and the *Lacey Act*[45].

While the NAFTA does not contain any mention of production process issues, article 10(2) of the NAFTA Environmental Supplement Agreement allows the Environmental Council to consider and develop recommendations on a large number of issues. These issues include "the environmental implications of goods throughout their lifecycle". Arguably, the Environ-

---

43 This was accomplished by ss. 20.2 to 20.4 of the *Crown Liability and Proceedings Act*.
44 Ernst-Ulrich Petersmann has provided a review of recent trade and environment issues at the GATT in his article "Trade Policy, Environmental Policy and the GATT: Why Trade Rules and Environmental Rules should be Mutually Consistent" *Aussenwirtshaft*, 46, Jahrgang (1991).
45 Testimony of Lori Wallach before the Senate Finance Committee, Sept. 26, 1993.

mental Council could consider the environmental effects of production processes on this basis.

(e) THE NADBANK AND BORDER ENVIRONMENT COOPERATION COMMISSION

During the debate over the ratification of the NAFTA in the United States, significant attention was lavished on the state of environmental infrastructure in the Mexican-American border zone. As a result of these concerns, the United States and Mexico created a Border Environment Cooperation Commission (Border Commission) and a North American Development Bank (NADBank)[46] to deal with environmental infrastructure projects along their border. The goals of these two institutions are to minimize any adverse environmental impact that may result from increased American-Mexican trade and to remedy existing environmental conditions along their border.

The Border Environment Cooperation Commission was created to work with affected border communities and Non-Governmental Organizations on border environmental issues. Its central function is to target monies towards environmental infrastructure projects, with initial preference to waste water, water treatment and solid waste projects. Headquartered in Ciudad Juarez, Mexico[47], the Border Commission will ensure that all projects meet minimum environmental and financial standards. The Border Commission is the only agency that can certify a project for NADBank funding. Project funding, however, need not be obtained only from the NADBank. Funding for projects may be obtained from other sources such as the World Bank or the Inter-American Development Bank.

By an exchange of letters, Mexico and the United States created the NADBank as a joint undertaking. Each country will subscribe for half of its capitalization which has been capped at US $3 billion[48]. The NADBank will be headquartered in San Antonio, Texas, with an adjunct office in Los Angeles[49], and will be governed by a six-member board. Mexico and the United States will each be entitled to appoint three members to the board. In addition to funding projects which have been certified by the Border Commission, the NADBank has a Community Adjustment Division, which will be able to distribute up to 10 percent of its initial capitalization on loans

---

46 *Agreement between the Government of the United States and Mexico Concerning the Establishment of a Border Environment Cooperation Commission and a North American Development Bank.*

47 *Inside Nafta*, Feb. 9, 1994 at 1.

48 §541 of the *North American Free Trade Agreement Implementation Act* authorized American subscription of up to US $1.5 billion.

49 *Inside Nafta*, Apr. 6, 1994 at 9.

and loan guarantees in each country to offset job losses and other detrimental NAFTA impacts.

3. WATER

Environmental and trade concerns have clashed on whether water, in its natural state, is subject to the obligations of the NAFTA. Some have viewed the NAFTA as guaranteeing unlimited transborder access to badly-needed fresh water resources. At the same time, to respond to concerns from environmental organizations, the governments of Canada and the United States have claimed that the NAFTA does not cover trade in water.

(a) DOES THE NAFTA COVER FRESH WATER?

NAFTA chapter 3 establishes obligations upon Parties regarding trade in goods. The Agreement defines goods as[50]:

> domestic products as these are understood in the *General Agreement on Tariffs and Trade* or such goods as the Parties may agree, and includes originating goods of that Party.

The GATT categorizes its products in its Harmonized Commodity Description and Coding System[51]. The system contains a tariff item for water, and it reads as follows:

> 22.01   waters, including natural or artificial waters and aerated waters, not containing added sugar or other sweetening matter nor flavouring; ice and snow.

There is an explanatory note with this tariff item. It states that the heading item covers "ordinary natural water of all kinds (other than sea water). Such water remains in this heading whether or not it is clarified or purified".

The item and its explanation include natural water in its solid state: snow and ice. Clearly, the GATT tariff item contemplates that unprocessed goods, such as snow and ice will be included in this category. On this basis, one must conclude that natural water will be treated as a good under the NAFTA, even when it is in its natural state[52]. Accordingly, the NAFTA will apply to ground and surface fresh water in its natural state.

---

50 NAFTA article 201.

51 *Harmonized Commodity Description and Coding System*, GATT, BISD, 34 Supp. 5 (1988) (L/6112, L/6222 and L/6292).

52 The U.S. Supreme Court in *Sporhase* v. *Nebraska*, 468 U.S. 941 (1982) has also concluded that ground water is an article of commerce for the purposes of the Commerce Clause in the U.S. Constitution. This grants Congress the constitutional power to regulate the international and interstate commerce of ground water.

The possibility that the NAFTA could impose obligations upon governmental water policy has concerned the Canadian government. In its *North American Free Trade Agreement Implementation Act,* Parliament included wording to prevent the NAFTA from applying to water policy. Section 7 of that Act states:

> (1) For greater certainty, nothing in this Act or the Agreement, except Article 302 of the Agreement[53], applies to water.
>
> (2) In this section, "water" means natural surface and ground water in liquid, gaseous or solid state, but does not include water packaged as a beverage or in tanks.

Under Canadian domestic law, the NAFTA does not apply to trade in surface or ground water. However, this definition is a matter of domestic law and is not binding on NAFTA panels. This statutory definition provides some understanding of the views of Canada, but cannot have an effect on how the international Agreement is interpreted.

The United States also suggests that the NAFTA does not apply to water policy, but takes a different approach. United States Trade Representative Mickey Kantor has written that "when water is traded as a good, all provisions of the agreements governing trade in goods apply"[54]. However, the "interbasin transfers of water in which water is not traded as a good are not governed by either trade agreement," (that is the Canada-U.S. Free Trade Agreement or the NAFTA).

Thus, in the American view, NAFTA's obligations on water will commence whenever water is traded as a good. This view appears to be an accurate reading of the terms of the NAFTA. When water is not traded as a good, it would not be subject to the terms of NAFTA chapter 3[55]. However, once water becomes traded, it would be covered by the NAFTA. While water is covered as a good, the NAFTA trade obligations will not apply until water is traded.

(b) WHAT OBLIGATIONS ARISE IF WATER IS TRADED?

The NAFTA incorporates the same national treatment obligation for goods as the GATT which requires that Parties provide national treatment

---

53 Article 302 deals with tariff elimination.

54 Letter of the United States Trade Representative Mickey Kantor to Nancy Newell, Oct. 28, 1993.

55 When water is not traded, it would be dealt with by other international agreements dealing with boundary waters such as the *Canada-U.S. Boundary Waters Agreement* of 1909 or the *Mexican-American Boundary Waters Treaty* of 1944.

for imported goods only[56]. This obligation does not speak to exported goods[57].

It has been suggested that the NAFTA national treatment obligation for goods is somehow modified by annex 301.3 which lists a number of export exceptions to this national treatment provision, including export controls on Canadian logs and unprocessed fish[58]. The listing of these exports as exceptions suggests that national treatment obligations could apply to export restrictions. However, since the underlying national treatment obligation speaks only to imported goods, this view cannot be correct.

(c) INVESTMENT OBLIGATIONS

Whether water is traded or not, the NAFTA Investment chapter imposes its obligations on how governments treat investors from other NAFTA Parties. These obligations cover the treatment of property rights such as water rights, or any other interest in land, which would enable trade in water to occur.

The NAFTA Investment chapter obliges governments to provide national treatment to the investments of investors of other NAFTA Parties with respect to the establishment, acquisition, expansion, management, conduct, operation and sale or other disposition of investments[59]. Unlike the national treatment obligation for goods, the Investment chapter's national treatment obligation does not treat exports differently from imports. NAFTA's investor rights will apply to all measures that limit water investments.

Should a NAFTA government prohibit the sale of water by a NAFTA investor, it would be possible for two different types of dispute settlements to occur. First, a NAFTA investor that found that its water rights were harmed by a government action could allege that an act of expropriation had occurred and claim compensation[60]. If compensation were not immediately forthcoming, then that investor could take that government to an investor-state arbitral tribunal. Alternatively, if the investor's government supported the complaint there could be a state-to-state dispute raised under the procedures laid out in NAFTA chapter 20.

---

56 NAFTA article 301.

57 GATT Article III:4.

58 For example, the Canadian Environmental Law Association has written "the inclusion of Annex 301.3 would seem to strongly suggest that NAFTA's National Treatment Provisions are not limited to imports, but, like the FTA, extend to exports as well." Wendy Holm in "Water and Free Trade" in *NAFTA and Water Exports* (Toronto: Canadian Environmental Law Association, October 1993) at 6.

59 NAFTA article 1102(2).

60 Pursuant to NAFTA article 1110.

(d) COULD A NAFTA GOVERNMENT BE REQUIRED TO SHIP FRESH WATER TO ANOTHER NAFTA PARTY UNDER THE TERMS OF THE AGREEMENT?

Governments could prevent the sale of fresh water to another country through the creation of export bans or by the imposition of prohibitive export charges on water exports. However, the NAFTA prohibits export prohibitions and restrictions against other Parties[61]. The Agreement also prohibits the imposition of export taxes, charges and duties against other NAFTA Parties unless these charges apply to all countries and are applied domestically[62]. Only if governments were prepared to impose prohibitive water consumption charges on their own could either of these approaches be permitted under the NAFTA.

Furthermore, NAFTA Parties are not able to rely upon the NAFTA's exceptions to freely prohibit exports. The NAFTA incorporates the GATT Article XX exceptions into its text[63]. These exceptions will apply to the trade in goods obligations in chapter 3, but not to the investment obligations of chapter 11. Thus, if governments prohibit water exports, they will not be able to insulate themselves from NAFTA investor-state tribunals or dispute settlement panels.

While governments could rely on the exhaustive natural resource exception contained in GATT Article XX(g), there is little reason to do so. The national treatment obligation contained in the Trade in Goods chapter does not apply to exports. Accordingly, export prohibitions would be justified in this chapter without relying on exceptions. Relying on this exemption would trigger other requirements. Whenever a government relies upon the natural resource exception, NAFTA article 315 incorporates the proportional sharing obligation of the Canada-U.S. Free Trade Agreement. It has the effect of banning preferential domestic pricing schemes. It also requires that proportional access of the resource be made available to the other Party on the basis of the average supply over the last 36-month period. Furthermore, the prior decisions of Canada-U.S. Free Trade panels which examined the use of the GATT Article XX(g) exception have held that this exception must only be used to the extent necessary and in proportion to the objective being served[64]. Thus, on the basis of the conditions imposed on the use of export bans by the NAFTA and arbitral decisions, if a Party decided to justify an export ban of fresh water for

---

61 NAFTA article 309.1.
62 NAFTA article 313.
63 NAFTA article 2101(1).
64 This decision, the *Salmon and Herring case*, was discussed more fully in chapter 21 of this book.

conservation reasons, that Party would be obligated to continue to supply other Parties on a proportional basis.

(e) CONCLUSION

The NAFTA's obligations are broad enough to cover natural surface and ground fresh water. The NAFTA chapter 3 national treatment obligation does not apply to water exports, but the investment obligations could require national treatment to be given to NAFTA investors who may have an investment in water.

NAFTA Parties are able to ban water exports but such an action could lead to valid challenges by affected NAFTA investors and their governments. The result of these challenges could result in damages or in the case of a chapter 20 panel, eventually, trade retaliation.

4. NAFTA AND THE ROLE OF THE STATE

Throughout its provisions, the NAFTA displays a classical liberal non-interventionist view on what constitutes an appropriate role for government. Speaking in the name of international certitude and market predictability, the NAFTA has established an international discipline on government behaviour towards business: limiting the scope of government activity in an attempt to create a level playing field. This view is manifested in a number of areas. Some examples include:

- provisions which require sanitary and phytosanitary measures to be justified on the basis of scientific criteria alone, and not on the basis of other legitimate government policy preferences;

- prohibitions imposed on all governments within the trade zone which end specific performance requirements in connection with the establishment or operation of a business by an investor of another NAFTA Party;

- restrictions on the policy-making capacity of the Parties, that reserved measures may never be changed in the future in a way that would make them more trade restrictive;

- an investor-state dispute-resolution system which creates a special system of adjudication available only to NAFTA investors where they can deal expeditiously with investment disputes against governments; and

- provisions which require government monopolies, at the federal level, to follow only commercial considerations when dealing with delegated authority from governments.

The NAFTA conception of the state leans towards one of the spectrum. Professor John Roberts identified a different prevalent conception of the role of the state in a contemporary liberal market democracy. He wrote[65]:

> essentially government's role reflects two imperatives. One is the need for some institution to act as an umpire in the clash of private interests in the society. The other is the need to assert the general interest of society — which is not the same as the sum of private interests as the market assesses them since there are economic and social costs attached to individual decisions which the free-market system excluded from the private-sector balance sheet.

This conception of the state is not entirely at odds with the conception contained within the NAFTA. The NAFTA acknowledges the desirability of the first of Professor Roberts' government roles. Indeed, throughout the NAFTA, provisions on government transparency and due process enhance the role of government as arbiter. However, the NAFTA strongly opposes a conception of government which takes an active role in the economy for economic, social or philosophical reasons.

Indeed, not only does the NAFTA constrain the existing capacity of the state, but in some ways it will act to limit future actions. The NAFTA locks-in fundamental economic reforms within each of the NAFTA Parties. Certainly, the NAFTA reduces the ability of governments to return to more protectionist economic policies which had been the hallmarks of earlier Canadian and Mexican governments. This prospective binding effect appears to have been particularly appealing to the government of Mexico. On this issue, political scientist Ian Robinson observed that[66]:

> one of the NAFTA's most important economic functions, in the Salinas administrations view, is to reduce national sovereignty by binding future Mexican governments to the privatization and liberalization strategy of the current government. The NAFTA would do this by embedding these policies in an international trade agreement that cannot be unilaterally re-negotiated and will be very costly and disruptive to abrogate.

This position, apparently taken by the government of Mexico on the role of the state in this Agreement, marks a substantive change in position. Traditionally, the three NAFTA countries had different political traditions

---

65 John Roberts, *Agenda for Canada: Towards a New Liberalism* (Toronto: Lester & Orpen Dennys, 1985) at 33-34.

66 Ian Robinson, *North American Trade as if Democracy Mattered: What's Wrong with NAFTA and What are the Alternatives* (Ottawa: Canadian Centre for Policy Alternatives, 1993) at 37.

and views on what constituted the appropriate role of the state. S.M. Lipset has commented on the difference in political culture between Canada and the United States. He suggests that the dominant traditions in Canada are statist and communitarian while those in the United States are anti-statist, individualistic and classically liberal[67]. Traditions in Mexico, while different, would be closer to the Canadian one.

In the debate over the benefits of the NAFTA, these divergent views were expressed. However, the final NAFTA Agreement establishes that only one view could prevail.

The NAFTA represents the supremacy of a classical liberal conception of the state with its imposition of significant restraints upon the role of government. All international trade agreements entail some self-imposed limitation on governmental authority, for example governments regularly agree not to increase their tariff rates. However, the NAFTA appears to approach an extreme. It does this by the extensiveness of its obligations which attempt to lock-in one perspective of governmental role for all successive North American governments. This must lead one to conclude that the NAFTA will mark the transformation of the predominently American view into the North American view.

---

67 S.M. Lipset, *Consensus and Conflict: Essays in Political Sociology* (New Brunswick: Transaction Books, 1985) as cited by Rod MacDonald "Tears are not Enough" in John D. Whyte and Ian Peach eds, *Re-Forming Canada? The Meaning of the Meech Lake Accord and the Free Trade Agreement for the Canadian State*. (Kingston: Institute of Intergovernmental Relations, Queen's University, 1989) at 10.

Index